741.2
Pea

Peach, Susan
    Technical drawing

900919

DATE DUE

TECHNICAL DRAWING

Susan Peach

Edited by Tony Potter

Consultant editor : Colin Rattray

(Lecturer at Middlesex Polytechnic
and freelance technical artist)

Technical consultant : Colin Motteram

Designed by Iain Ashman

Illustrated by Chris Lyon

Additional illustrations by
Guy Smith, Peter Bull,
Mick Posen, Martin Newton,
Steve Cross and Jeremy Gower.

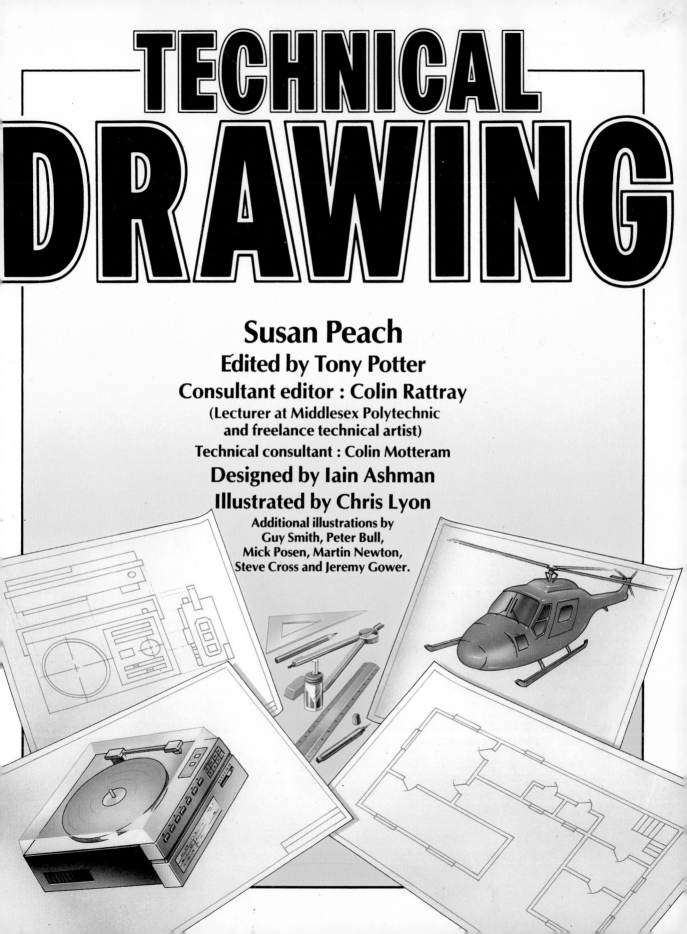

Contents

First published in 1987 by Usborne Publishing Ltd, 20
Garrick Street, London, WC2E 9BJ, England.
Copyright © 1987 Usborne Publishing Ltd.

Printed in Great Britain.   American edition 1987.

About this book

This book is a guide to technical drawing and illustration for beginners.

It shows the stages involved in designing and drawing objects, starting with rough sketches and models. You can also find out about special methods of drawing, called orthographic and isometric projections and perspective.

To start with, you do not need any special equipment – just a ruler and pencils. A smooth table top will do as a drawing board.

At the back of the book you can find out about more complicated drawing equipment, and about common abbreviations and symbols used to simplify drawings.

You can also find out how to colour and mount your drawings for displays and exhibitions, and how to use photographs.

Glossary

Technical drawing is full of unusual words. These are explained in the glossary on page 47, and are highlighted in the book each time you come across them, like this: *isometric*.

What is technical drawing?

Perspective drawing

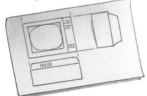

Orthographic projection

Technical drawing is a means of communicating instructions and information to people to help them make or build things, or imagine how they will look when made.

Some sorts of technical drawings, such as *perspective drawings*, give general information about what an object actually looks like.

Other drawings, like *orthographic projections*, give precise information about the size and shape of an object, so that someone could make it from the instructions on the drawing.

In technical drawing a series of rules, called *conventions*, are used to simplify the drawings and to ensure that they are easily understood. This means that a drawing can be passed from one person to another, or even sent to another country where a different language is used, and still be understood.

Who uses technical drawings?

Technical drawings are widely used in all the professions which involve designing, building or making objects. They are used to pass detailed technical information about the size, shape and construction of an object from the designer to the person who will make the object.

Architects and civil engineers use technical drawings to show builders how to construct a building and what materials to use.

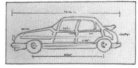

Mechanical engineers use technical drawings to pass instructions to the factory about how to make their designs.

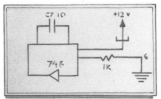

Electronic engineers do technical drawings to design circuits and show how they are wired up.

Product designers produce technical drawings to show clients what their ideas will look like when the product is made.

Getting started

You do not have to spend a lot of money on technical drawing equipment, as the basic tools and equipment, shown below, are simple and cheap. All you need is a flat surface to work on (a desk or table), a plastic ruler, compasses, 60°/30° and 45° triangles, a protractor, some sharp pencils, masking tape and paper.

If you want to invest in some more specialized equipment, there are suggestions below for professional tools to buy and how to use them.

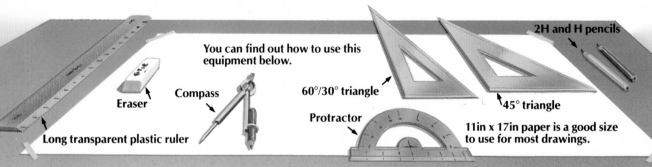

You can find out how to use this equipment below.

Eraser

Compass

Long transparent plastic ruler

60°/30° triangle

Protractor

45° triangle

2H and H pencils

11in x 17in paper is a good size to use for most drawings.

Drawing board and T-square

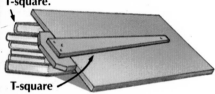

Prop the board on some books to give clearance for the T-square.

T-square

Masking tape

Cover your board with thick paper to give a smooth surface.

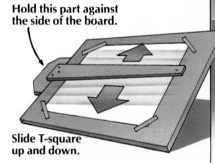

Hold this part against the side of the board.

Slide T-square up and down.

Two additional pieces of equipment are useful: a drawing board and a T-square. These are not very expensive and they make technical drawing much easier to do.

You could make your own board from plywood (available from builders' merchants), but make sure at least one of the edges is cut straight and smooth to take the T-square.

A T-square is used to draw horizontal lines and as a support for triangles. Slide the T-square to the position you want, hold it still and draw along its top edge.

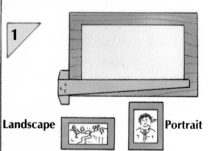

1

Landscape Portrait

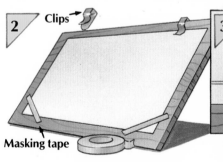

2

Clips

Masking tape

3

Title block

Name:
Title: Scale:

To get the paper straight on the board, move the T-square to the bottom of the board and line the paper up against it. There are two ways of positioning paper, shown above.

The paper has to be attached to the board so that it does not move around while you are drawing. You can do this with masking tape, sticky tape or drawing board clips.

Your drawing will look neater if you pencil in a border line ½in from the edge, and a title block to show your name, the title and scale of the drawing.

Paper

Various types of paper are used for technical drawing. Bond or construction paper is used for pencil drawings and plans. Tracing paper is used with marker pens and for tracing over photos. You can find out about different sizes of paper on page 38.

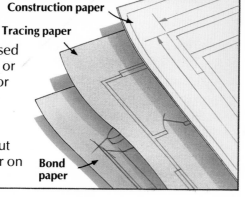

Construction paper
Tracing paper
Bond paper

Triangles and protractor

Triangles are used to draw lines at 90°, 60°, 45° and 30°, angles which are frequently needed. Triangles are made of transparent plastic so that you can see the drawing underneath. You will need two: a 45° and a 60°/30° triangle.

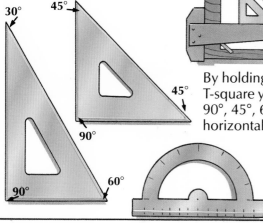

30°
45°
90°
90°
60°

Lines at 90°
Lines at 45°

By holding a triangle against the T-square you can draw lines at 90°, 45°, 60° and 30° to the horizontal.

45°
45°

You also need a protractor to measure other angles.

Compasses

Compasses are used to draw *arcs* and circles. You can use an ordinary compass, but a spring bow compass, shown on the right, is best as it can not slip out of position.

To avoid the compass point slipping or making holes in the paper, stick a piece of masking tape over the centre of the circle to be drawn. This will hold the point in position.

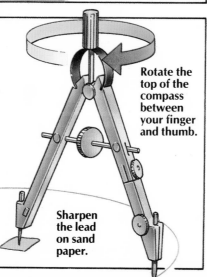

Rotate the top of the compass between your finger and thumb.

Sharpen the lead on sand paper.

Pencils and pens

Pencils come in different hardnesses*, H or 2H pencils are best for drawing with instruments, while softer HB or 2B pencils are good for drawing freehand. Pencils must be kept sharp to draw fine and accurate lines.

A pencil sharpener gives a sharp round point.

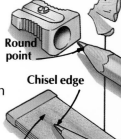

Round point

You can also rub the lead on sand paper to get a chisel edge, which draws a very fine line.

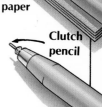

Chisel edge
Sand paper

Clutch pencils are useful, as they do not need to be sharpened.

Clutch pencil

To do ink line drawings you need a technical pen with a point thickness of about 0.2mm.

Technical pen

Other useful things

Pair of dividers

Liquid cleanser for cleaning tools.

Art gum

You will find information about more complicated drawing equipment on page 38-39.

Stages in design

To get from an initial idea to a finished product, there are several design stages. This is often called the *design process*. As part of this process, a designer uses technical drawings to illustrate and explain ideas.

These pages show a flow chart of the nine main stages involved. A designer does not have to go through all the stages, or always in the same order.

You could try designing something at home to see how the design process works. As an example there are some tips on these pages for designing a cassette rack, but you can use the same stages for anything you design.

Flow chart

The chart below is a summary of the main stages in the design process. Follow the arrows below and on these pages to see different routes you can take.

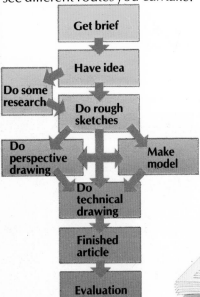

The brief

First, someone (called the client) asks a designer to design something. The client gives the designer a brief – a set of instructions about what the design will be used for, what it must look like and how much it can cost.

A written brief

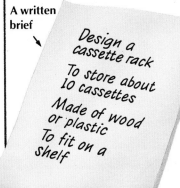

Design a cassette rack
To store about 10 cassettes
Made of wood or plastic
To fit on a shelf

Research

The designer has to know how the object being designed is to be made, as this helps work out the details. Designers often consult with engineers and other experts, or do research to discover what they need to know.

At home, this could mean borrowing books from the library and reading up on the subject.

The idea

Designers come up with ideas for the design which follow the brief. They think about what the object will be used for and what it could look like.

You could get ideas for your design from shops or pictures in magazines.

Sketches

Ideas are often developed as small rough sketches (called *thumbnails*). Lots of ideas can be quickly tried out until one is found that works.

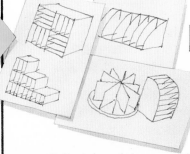

You will find that doing pencil sketches of the cassette rack helps you work out your ideas.

Find out more about sketching on pages 8-9.

Perspective drawing

Designers often do a realistic three-dimensional picture of their design, called a *perspective* drawing. This is cheaper and quicker than making a model, but still shows the client how the product will look.

You may find a perspective drawing useful to show other people what your rack looks like.

Find out how to do perspective drawings on pages 24-27.

Technical drawing

Technical drawings convey precise information about an object's size and shape to the person who will make it. The plans that the designer has drawn up are passed on to someone else (like a builder, carpenter or engineer) to show them how to make the design.

At home, technical drawings are the most accurate way of working out the details of something you want to make, such as its shape and sizes, called *dimensions*.

Orthographic projection

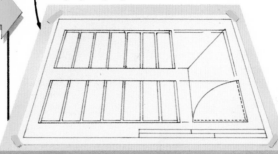

You can find out how to do orthographic projections on pages 14-19.

Orthographic projections show the different sides of an object, all drawn facing the viewer. They also give exact information about its size and how the parts fit together.

Isometric projection

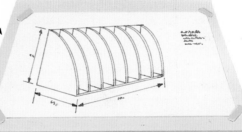

You can find out how to do isometric projections on pages 22-23.

Isometric projections are three-dimensional, and are used to give accurate scale measurements of an object.

Model

Making a model is an easy way of testing that a design works. Designers often make models (called *mock-ups*) to show clients how the finished product will look.

To try out your rack you could make a mock-up from card. This helps check that the parts fit together.

Your model can be full-size or to scale.

You can find how to make card models like this on pages 10-13.

The finished article and evaluation

Next the article is made. The final stage of the design process is called evaluation. This is when the designer assesses how successful the design has been – if it has fulfilled the brief and if it could be improved.

Sketching

When you have an idea for something to design, the first stage is often to do some quick freehand sketches of what you want it to look like. Professional designers often do lots of tiny sketches, called *thumbnails*, to try out their ideas.

On these pages you can find out how a sketch can be useful, whatever you are designing, and read some tips on making sketching easier.

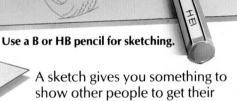

Examples of sketches

Use a B or HB pencil for sketching.

Why do a sketch?

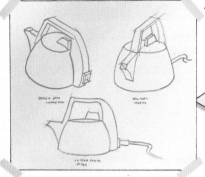

Sketching helps to sort out your ideas – you can quickly try out different designs to see which looks best.

A sketch is good preparation for more complicated technical drawings. It helps work out the *layout** on the page.

A sketch gives you something to show other people to get their advice on your ideas.

Sketching tips

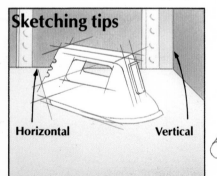

Horizontal   Vertical

Start your drawing with any vertical and horizontal lines in the surroundings, as these act as reference points for the rest of the drawing.

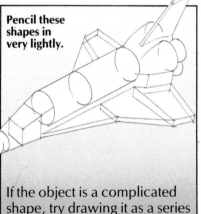

Pencil these shapes in very lightly.

If the object is a complicated shape, try drawing it as a series of boxes and cylinders. Sketch these shapes in first as a framework for the outline.

This is called negative space.

Remember to look at the space around the object as well. Think about the object's position in relation to its surroundings.

*The layout is the arrangement of a drawing on the paper.

Sketching from start to finish

When you design something you often need to sketch it from your imagination. Drawing real objects is good practice for this.

Here you can find out how to go about doing a sketch, from start to finish. A telephone is used as an example, but you could sketch any object.

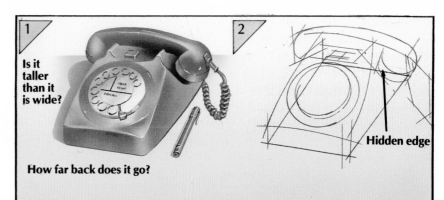

1 Is it taller than it is wide?

How far back does it go?

Before you start, look carefully at the object and work out its proportions. This helps you to get the shape right in your sketch.

2 Hidden edge

Pencil in a rough framework with *construction lines**. Show the position of hidden edges, as this helps to get the proportions right.

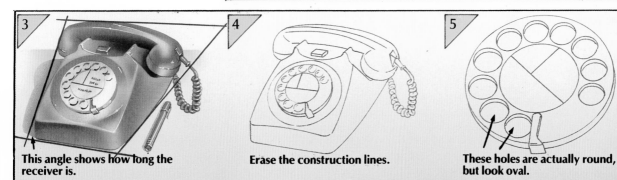

3 This angle shows how long the receiver is.

Imagine lines at angles between various parts of the object to help you check the size and proportion of the parts in relation to one another.

4 Erase the construction lines.

For a rough sketch you may not need to draw more than the main outline. If you want to add details, such as the dial holes, do this last.

5 These holes are actually round, but look oval.

Look at the object repeatedly while you are drawing to check what you see. Always draw what you see, not what you know the object looks like.

Getting the proportions right

If you work on a drawing for a long time you may not notice any errors building up, so it is best to check the shape and proportions regularly.

Try squinting at your drawing or looking at it in the mirror to get a new view.

Try not to press too hard with the pencil until you are happy with the proportions.

A good way to judge proportions is to measure your object with a pencil, as shown on the right.

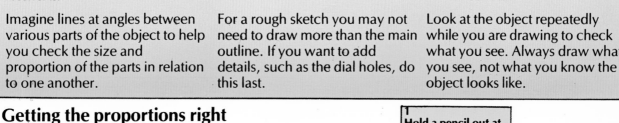

1 Hold a pencil out at arm's length and shut one eye.

2 Line up the pencil with a short upright or horizontal edge on the subject.

3 "Mark" the length on the pencil with your thumb.

4 Keep your thumb still, and count how many times this length fits into other lengths on the object.

5 Check that the proportions are the same on your sketch.

**These are faint lines used to construct the rough shape before you draw the outline.

Models

Designers often produce models, called *mock-ups*, to check that their design works and to show their clients. On these pages you can find out how to make a cube from paper or thin card, and how to adapt it to make other exciting models, like a house and a truck. The models are made from *developments*, which are plans showing all the sides of an object opened out on to one *plane* (surface).

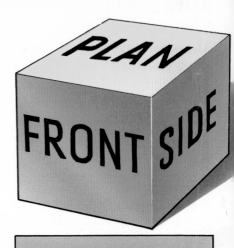

Making a cube

Things you will need:

- Strong glue
- Sharp craft knife or Exacto-knife
- Piece of 8½in x 11in card or paper

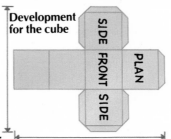

Development for the cube

SIDE
FRONT
PLAN
SIDE

Keep the cube – you will be able to use it on page 15.

1

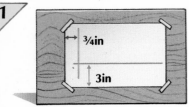

¾in

3in

Fix the card to your drawing board with masking tape. Make sure that the card is square to the board. With a 2H pencil, draw a horizontal line 3in up from the bottom of the card, and a vertical one from ¾in from the left-hand side.

2

Measure each square from line A to stop errors building up.

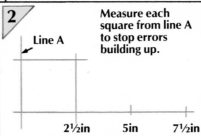

Line A

2½in   5in   7½in

Where the lines cross, measure 2½in to the right and 2½in up. Using a T-square and triangle, complete the square. Add on the remaining five squares, as shown on the development.

3

PLAN

Centre lines to position lettering.

Draw in tabs ½in wide for sticking the cube together as shown on the development. (Note: if you want to use the cube on page 15, write "Front", "Side" and "Plan" on the faces shown.)

4

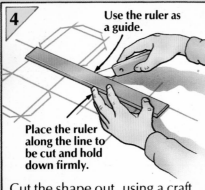

Use the ruler as a guide.

Place the ruler along the line to be cut and hold down firmly.

Cut the shape out, using a craft knife or an Exacto-knife. Score along all the lines to be bent by running the knife over them once only.

5

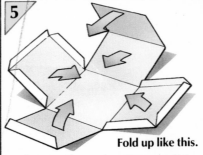

Fold up like this.

Colour in the cube. You could use marker pens – there are some tips on how to use them on page 29. Then fold the cube along the scored lines and glue it together.

A gift box

The cube can easily be adapted to make a gift box. The arrangement of the tabs on the development above is slightly different, as you will need tabs on the lid to hold the box closed, as shown below.

Development for the gift box

Making a truck

The developments for the truck below are on page 45. Enlarge* them on to construction paper, paint or colour them, then cut out the pieces.

1
Fold up and glue the cab together.

2
Fold up and glue the container in the same way as the cube.

3
Bend this tab outwards.

4
Fold up the base and glue it together at the corners.

5
Fold the corners like this.

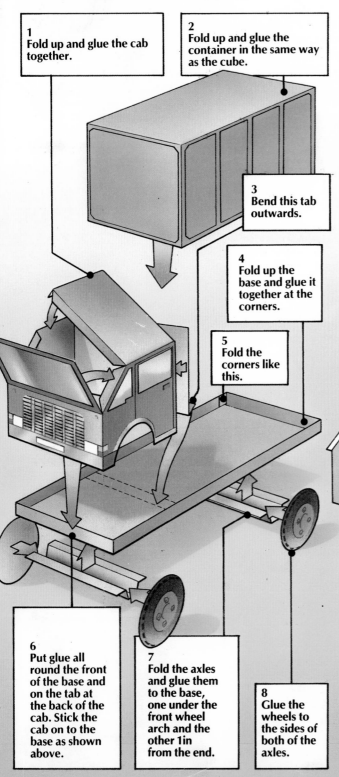

6
Put glue all round the front of the base and on the tab at the back of the cab. Stick the cab on to the base as shown above.

7
Fold the axles and glue them to the base, one under the front wheel arch and the other 1in from the end.

8
Glue the wheels to the sides of both of the axles.

Making a house

1
Copy the developments from page 44 and enlarge* them on to construction paper. If you want to colour the model, do it while it is flat. Then cut out the pieces with a knife.

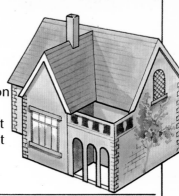

2
Glue here.

Bend back the tabs at the bottom of the house and porch walls and glue them to the inside to reinforce the base.

3
Fold the walls and glue them together. Fold the roof and glue it to the walls. You could leave the model like this and make it a cottage.

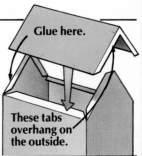

Glue here.

These tabs overhang on the outside.

4
Stick on here.

Fold up the porch walls and glue the tabs on to the front wall. Fold up the porch roof and glue it on to the porch walls and the roof.

5
Cut out the balcony arches, leaving the flap at the bottom as a support. Fold and glue the tabs to the main building.

Glue on here.

6
Fold up the chimney and glue it together. Glue the chimney to the porch roof.

You can find out how to enlarge the plans on page 46.

Modelling tips

Models can be made from a variety of different materials. The models shown here are made from cheap and simple things that you may have at home.

On these pages you can find out about some of the techniques used for working with card, Plasticine and polystyrene. These tips will help you to make simple models of your own designs.

Successful model-making depends on accurate measurements and cutting, so it is best to work out things like the scale and the shape of parts first.

Construction kits

Construction kits are useful for making quick and simple models of your designs, and do not require any special techniques or artistic ability to make effective, good-looking models.

Special components like doors, windows and wheels make models of buildings and vehicles even easier to do. You can also use these parts for the other models described on these pages.

Plasticine

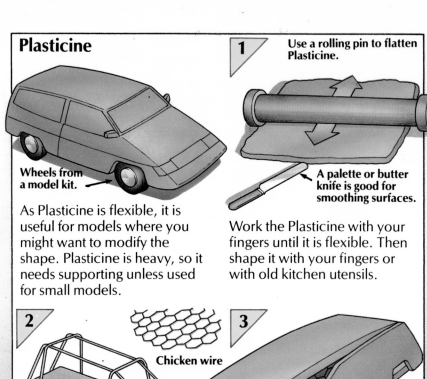

Wheels from a model kit.

As Plasticine is flexible, it is useful for models where you might want to modify the shape. Plasticine is heavy, so it needs supporting unless used for small models.

1 Use a rolling pin to flatten Plasticine.

A palette or butter knife is good for smoothing surfaces.

Work the Plasticine with your fingers until it is flexible. Then shape it with your fingers or with old kitchen utensils.

2

Chicken wire

Chicken wire is useful for larger models as it is light and strong.

Large models need a hidden skeleton, called an armature, to support them. Armatures can be made from things like wood, wire or cardboard.

3

Armature

Make the armature the rough size and shape of the model, cover it with Plasticine and then mould the material to the final shape.

Polystyrene

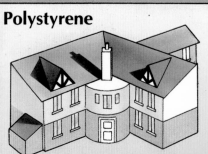

Expanded polystyrene is good for making simple models that can be carved from a block. You can use blocks of polystyrene packing material.

1

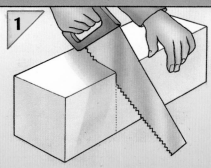

Polystyrene can be easily cut with wood-working tools like saws and rasps. Smaller details can be cut with an Exacto-knife or craft knife.

Card

You can make complicated models like this spaceship by glueing a series of card *developments* together. It is best to sketch out the development first, to work out where to join the sides together and put tabs.

Make this part from an ice lolly stick.

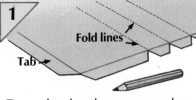

1

Fold lines

Tab

Draw the development on the card. To glue the model together there must be a tab on one side of any two edges to be joined.

2

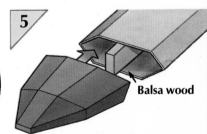

Score folds on the outside of the model.

Before you glue your model together, score all fold lines with the back of the blade of a craft knife, using a ruler as a straight edge.

3

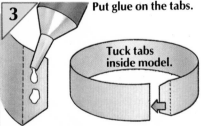

Put glue on the tabs.

Tuck tabs inside model.

Paper clips are useful for holding the pieces in place while the glue dries. When it has set, use a knife to remove any blobs of glue on the outside of the model.

4

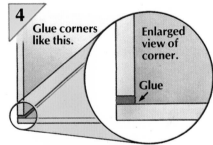

Glue corners like this.

Enlarged view of corner.

Glue

If you are using thick card which will not fold easily, it is better to cut the sides out separately and then stick them together as shown above.

5

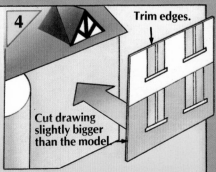

Balsa wood

Larger card and paper models may need a support to keep them rigid. A good support can be made from thin strips of balsa wood glued inside the card model.

2

You can use a wire brush to make any curved shapes. Use the brush to work away the surface of the block and create a curve.

3

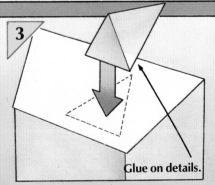

Glue on details.

To glue several pieces of polystyrene together, you must use a non-solvent glue* as other glues dissolve the surface of polystyrene.

4

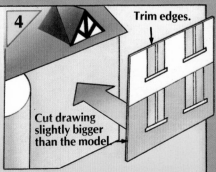

Trim edges.

Cut drawing slightly bigger than the model

A good way to finish polystyrene models is to do a suitable drawing on paper, then glue it to the surface of the model.

Such as Copydex or a polystyrene cement.

Orthographic projection

Orthographic projection is a method of drawing an object by producing a series of flat views of its different sides. This means that all the object's features can be shown. Each side is seen in its true shape, unlike *perspective drawings*, which distort the view. Orthographic projections are used by engineers and architects to show detailed instructions about an object, so that it can be reproduced exactly.

There are six possible views of any object (see below), but three are usually enough to show all the features. These three views are called the *front*, *side* and *plan* views. The front and side can also be called the front and side *elevations*.

The views are positioned on the page in a fixed *layout*. There are two kinds of layout, called *first angle* and *third angle*. You can read about first angle below, and third angle on page 18-19.

Engineers and architects agree to draw things in either first or third angle in order to avoid any confusion when drawings are passed from one person to another – from the designer to the engineer, for example. All orthographic projections are marked to tell the viewer which layout has been used. The symbols used are:

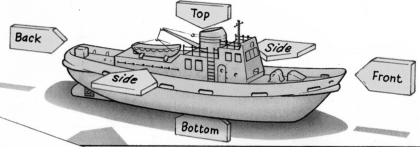

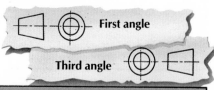

First angle projection

In first angle projection, the drawings are always laid out as shown below.

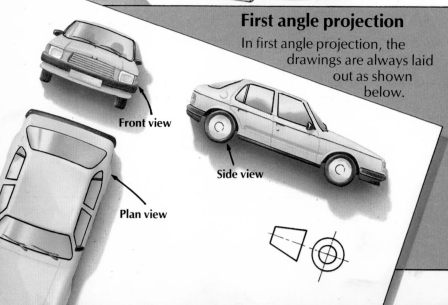

Front view

Side view

Plan view

Lots of objects do not have an obvious front, side or top. You will have to choose which side is to be which, but try to position the object so that the maximum amount of information can be shown in the three views.

First angle was the traditional method used in Europe. But nowadays Europeans use either first or third angle, so all drawings must be labelled to show which layout is being used.

First angle drawings

Follow the steps below to find out why the views are laid out as they are for first angle projection. You will need:

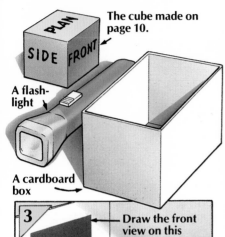

The cube made on page 10.

A flash-light

A cardboard box

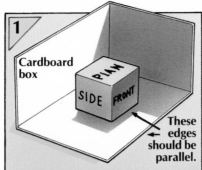

1

Cardboard box

These edges should be parallel.

Cut up a cardboard box to leave two sides and the base. Stand the cube inside the box with the plan face on top and the front and side faces towards you.

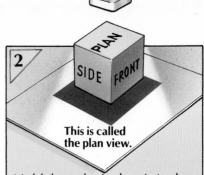

2

This is called the plan view.

Hold the cube in the air and shine a flashlight on the top face so that its shadow falls on the base of the box. This is where the view of the top face will be. Put the cube back on the base of the box and draw round it.

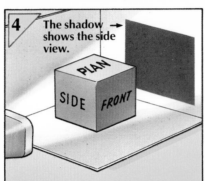

3

Draw the front view on this wall.

Shine the flashlight on to the front face of the cube so the shadow is projected on to the box wall behind. The shadow shows the front view position.

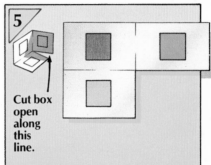

4

The shadow shows the side view.

Shine the flashlight on to the side face, so that its shadow is projected behind. Draw round the cube again. This is called the side or end view.

5

Cut box open along this line.

Cut the box open as shown and flatten it out. You can now see how the views are arranged on paper. They are always set out in the same pattern, so they do not need labels.

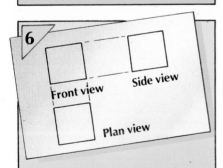

6

Front view   **Side view**

Plan view

The separate views are always shown in line with each other. Spaces are left between them for *dimensions* (length, breadth and other measurements)and other notes.

Drawing other objects

As all the cube's sides are the same shape, all the views are the same. Try sketching another object with sides of different shapes, using the steps shown above.

On your drawing the left side will be shown to the right of the front view.

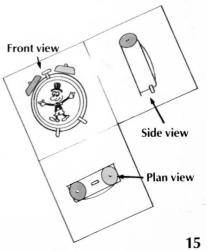

Front view

Side view

Plan view

First angle orthographic projection

Follow the steps shown on these pages to draw a *first angle* orthographic projection of any object. A cassette box is shown as an example, but the same method is used to do accurate drawings of anything, either a real object or something you are designing from your own imagination.

1 **Before you start**

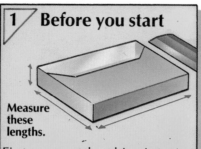

Measure these lengths.

First measure the object's length, width and height, as well as any other *dimensions* that will be needed. Note them on a piece of scrap paper.

2

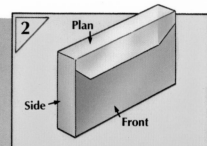

Plan

Side

Front

Decide which side is to be the *front*, which the *side* and which the *plan* view. It does not really matter which is which, as long as all the features are shown.

3

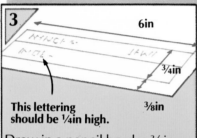

6in

¾in

⅜in

This lettering should be ¼in high.

Draw in a pencil border ⅜in from the edges of the paper and a title block* in the bottom right-hand corner. The title block should show the title and *scale* of the drawing, your name and the date.

4 **Always state which units you are using.**

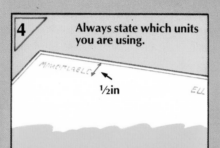

½in

You must state that you are using first angle projection and that the dimensions are in inches. Write this on a line at the top of the paper or in the title block.

5

Divide up these spaces equally.

Work out the position of the views on the page. They need to be evenly spaced, not squashed up on one side. It is a good idea to do a sketch first to work out the rough *layout*.

Drawing to scale

It is not always possible to do full-size orthographic projections. Sometimes you will have to draw an object to scale – either larger or smaller than real life.

The scale is usually written as a *ratio* (a mathematical way of showing the proportion of one quantity to another). For example, if the drawing is half the size of the real object, the scale is written 1:2 – every one unit in the drawing represents two units in real life. If the drawing is five times as big as the object, the scale is 5:1.

You must tell the viewer the scale by showing the ratio in the title block.

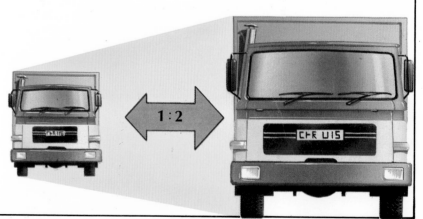

1 : 2

Doing the drawing

Lines

Different parts of the drawing are done in different lines*. The main ones are:

Construction lines – faint continuous lines used to plot out the basic shapes and for *projection* and *dimension lines* (see below). Use a 4H pencil.

Outlines – firm continuous lines used to show the outline of the object. Outlines are often drawn over construction lines. Use a 2H pencil.

1
Measure basic dimensions (height and length) for the front view. Using a 4H pencil, draw construction lines right across the page and down too.

2
Measure and draw construction lines for the width of the side view and the height of the plan view.

3
Go over the outlines with a 2H pencil. Press quite hard so that the outlines stand out clearly.

Units of dimension

Construction line

Outline

Angle of projection

Title box

Border line

4
Draw in dimension lines with a 2H pencil. Dimension lines have an arrowhead at each end, and the point of the arrow should touch the projection line.

5
Projection lines are used to position the dimension lines outside the outline. They start about ⅛in outside the outline and extend just beyond the dimension line. You can often draw them on top of the construction lines.

6
Write dimensions in the centre of the dimension lines. The figures should be ⅛-¼in high.

Arrowheads must be drawn like this: ◄―

not like this: ←

Lettering

Lettering in the title block and elsewhere on the drawing is normally done in capital letters. Small letters are only used in abbreviations**, and are done in printed writing.

Letters should be the same height: about ¼in.

FULL SIZE

Pencil in guide lines to keep the letters neat.

Rub-down lettering looks neat. Rub each letter with the blunt end of a pencil to transfer it to your paper.

Rounded letters like o, b and p are larger than other letters, and need to sit just below the guideline to look even with other letters.

Spaces between letters should look the same size, even though they actually vary.

1st tool box

These letters should sit below the line.

Remove mistakes by sticking a piece of masking tape over the letter, then peeling the tape and the letter off gently.

*There is more information on the lines used in technical drawing on page 42.
**There is a list of common abbreviations on page 42.

Third angle orthographic projection

These pages explain *third angle projection*, which is the most commonly used *layout*. Third angle is an alternative method of viewing an object to *first angle*.

Originally third angle was used in North America, but nowadays it is used in Europe too. First and third angle projections are equally acceptable and approved internationally.

Origin of first and third angle

In geometry, each of the four *quadrants* formed by the intersecting *planes* in the diagram is called one "angle". Those numbered 1 and 3 are used in *orthographic projection*.

Imagine that the object to be drawn is suspended in either the first or third angle. The *front* and *plan* views are projected on to the planes, which are then opened out in the direction of the arrows to give the layouts for first and third angle.

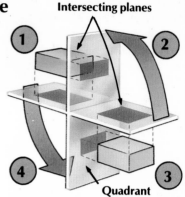

Intersecting planes

Quadrant

The use of the first and third angles rather than the second or fourth is just a *convention*.

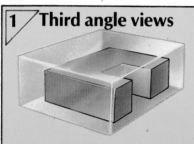

1 Third angle views

You can see how a third angle projection is laid out by imagining that the object to be drawn is suspended in the middle of a glass box.

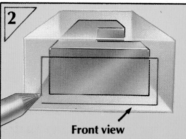

2

Front view

If you looked through each side of the box in turn you could draw on the glass the front, *side* and plan views of the object inside.

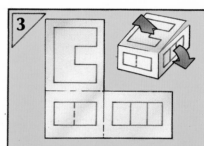

3

If the glass box were cut open and flattened out, you would end up with three views arranged as above. This is third angle layout.

Symbols

The symbols used to show which layout is being used are themselves orthographic projections. The symbols show the front and side views of a cone with the end cut off. In each case the side view shows the left-hand or narrower end of the object.

The first angle symbol shows the side view projected to the right of the front view.

First angle

The third angle symbol shows it in its true position : to the left of the front view.

Third angle

Advantages of third angle

In third angle the side and plan views are drawn in the same relationship to the front view as they are in real life : the plan is drawn above, and the side view is drawn at the side it represents. This makes third angle layout easier to understand, which is why it is becoming more widely used than first angle.

This side view shows the left-hand side of the object. It is drawn to the left of the front view.

The plan view, which shows the top of the object, is drawn above the front view.

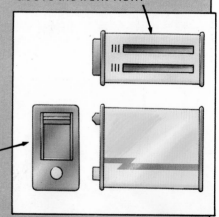

Third angle drawings

Apart from the layout, third angle drawings are done in the same way as first angle, with construction lines, outlines and so on. The tips below show you how to draw things like circular parts and hidden details.

Thin dashed lines like this are used to draw any hidden details which need to be shown, like the position of the batteries.

This side view shows the right-hand side of the radio, and in third angle is drawn to the right of the front view.

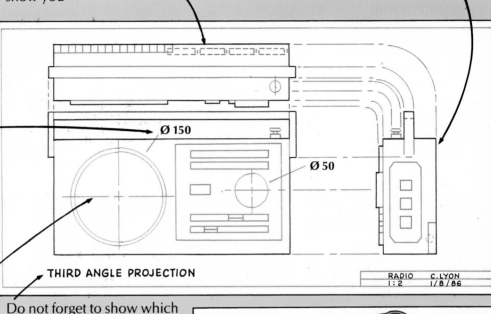

Ø 150

Ø 50

THIRD ANGLE PROJECTION

RADIO   C. LYON
1:2   1/8/86

Dimensions of circular parts are shown like this. Do not use the *centre lines* as *dimension lines*. On the drawing, diameter is often abbreviated to ø.

Find the centre of circular parts by drawing two centre lines (thin *chain lines* with alternate long and short dashes) crossing at 90° where the centre is to be. Centre lines should not cross in the spaces between dashes, and they should extend outside the outline of the circle.

Do not forget to show which layout you are using.

Things to draw

You could practise drawing orthographic projections with other objects like these.

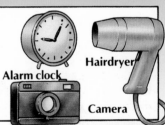

Alarm clock

Hairdryer

Camera

Orthographic projection puzzles

Here are some unusual views of household objects. See if you can work out what the objects are and which orthographic view is shown.*

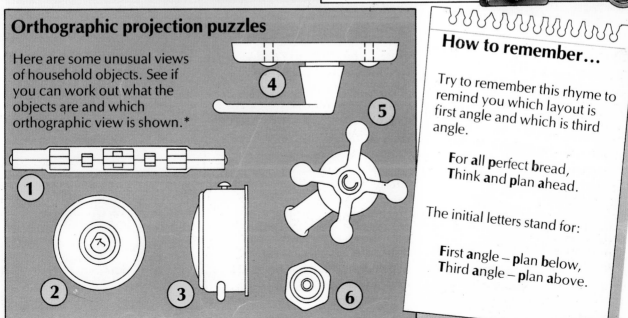

How to remember...

Try to remember this rhyme to remind you which layout is first angle and which is third angle.

For **a**ll **p**erfect **b**read,
Think **a**nd **p**lan **a**head.

The initial letters stand for:

First angle – **p**lan **b**elow,
Third angle – **p**lan **a**bove.

Architectural drawing

Orthographic *plan views* are often used by builders and architects to show the *layout* of buildings. They have special symbols to show common features like doors, windows and stairs. On these pages you can find out how to draw simple architectural plans using these symbols. Once you have mastered the basic *conventions*, you can use them to design your own exciting buildings.

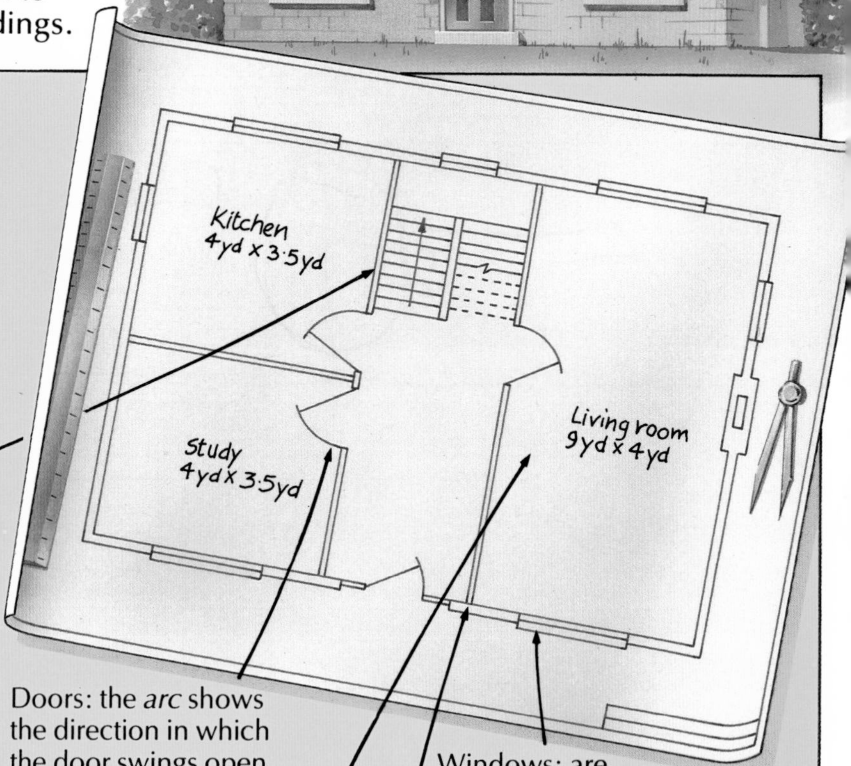

Architectural conventions

This is an architectural plan of the ground floor of the house shown above. It is the kind of plan that builders use to lay out the foundations. On the plan you can see some of the common architectural features, and how to represent them.

Stairs: The length of the staircase should be divided up equally into the number of stairs, as shown below. The stairs are numbered from the bottom and arrows are drawn to show the "up" direction.

Kitchen
4 yd x 3.5 yd

Study
4 yd x 3.5 yd

Living room
9 yd x 4 yd

How to space stairs

Top of stairs

Bottom of stairs

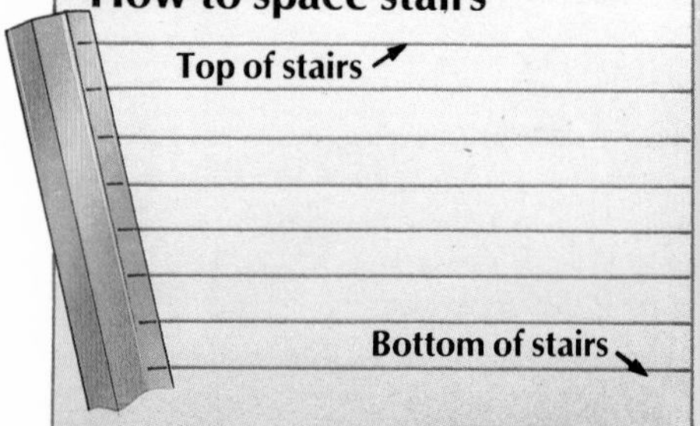

Here is how to divide up the space occupied by a staircase into (for example) seven stairs. Angle a ruler with the 0 at the top of the stairs and 3½in on the bottom, as shown above. Mark off every ½in between the top and bottom. Draw parallel lines through the marks to divide up the space into seven stairs.

Doors: the *arc* shows the direction in which the door swings open. Draw it with a pair of compasses.

Dimensions: the room *dimensions* show the internal measurements from wall to wall, but do not include the thickness of the walls.

Walls: there are two main types of walls – outer walls and internal partitions. Partitions are usually built about 4½in thick, while outer walls are much thicker (about 12in).

Windows: are drawn like this.

Scale: Architectural plans are always drawn to *scale*, which must be shown clearly on the drawing. A scale of 1:36 is easy to use, as each inch on the drawing will represent a yard (3ft) in real life. You can find out more about scale on page 16.

To practise drawing house plans, you could copy this plan using your drawing equipment.

1 Draw your home

Before you start, measure the lengths of the walls in all the rooms to be shown. To do this you need a long tape measure, such as a dressmaker's or carpenter's tape.

2

Note the position and width of windows and doors, and which way the doors open. If your home is on more than one floor, remember to show the stairs.

3

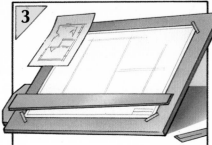

Next do a rough sketch to help you work out a suitable scale and page layout. Then you can do the final drawing with your equipment. Remember to show the scale.

Design your own buildings

You could try drawing plans of imaginary buildings, such as your ideal house, a farm, a fairy tale castle or a space station.

Here are the conventional ways of drawing some other features which you might like to include on your plans.

Sink
Bath
Spiral staircase
Range
Toilet
Basin

Try drawing front and side views to go with your plans. In architecture these are called *elevations*. Normally all four elevations are shown: front, back and both sides. They are usually named after the direction they face, such as the north elevation. Elevations do not have to be drawn in any special layout – just arranged neatly on the page.

You can see below how to show doors and windows on elevations.

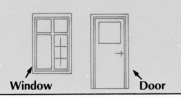

Window   Door

Puzzle

See if you can work out and draw the layout of the flat described on the right.

To find out if you were correct, look at the actual layout on page 46.

Small & Pricey Ltd.
Estate Agents

The apartment has a total area of 12yd x 8½yd. All the rooms have windows looking out over the front or back yards.

The front door enters the L-shaped hall, from which all the rooms lead. On the left is the living room (6yd x 5½yd). A door from the living room leads into the kitchen (4yd x 3yd), which overlooks the back yard. Next to the kitchen is the bathroom (3½yd x 2yd). The main bedroom (5½yd x 4½yd) is situated at the front of the house, while the second bedroom (4½yd x 3½yd) overlooks the yard.

21

Isometric drawing

From an *orthographic projection*, it can be difficult to imagine what the object really looks like. To help visualize things, engineers and architects use a style of three-dimensional drawing, called *isometric projection*. Isometric projections are useful because they are quick and easy to draw.

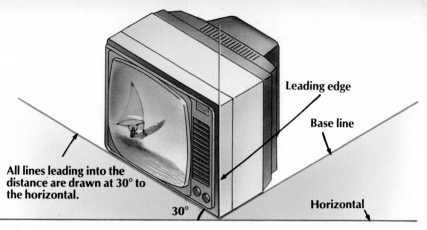

Leading edge

Base line

All lines leading into the distance are drawn at 30° to the horizontal.

30°

Horizontal

The drawing above shows an isometric projection of a TV. Isometric drawings are not in *perspective*, so they look slightly distorted. Their advantage is that all the sides of an object are drawn at their true length, so you can take measurements from the finished drawing.

How to do an isometric drawing

These steps show how to do an isometric drawing. A video is shown, but you could draw any box-shaped object. Note down the object's measurements before you start.

Use a scale if the object is too big or small to be drawn full-size.

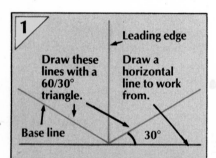

1

Leading edge

Draw these lines with a 60/30° triangle.

Draw a horizontal line to work from.

Base line

30°

Draw a vertical line for the *leading edge* (the edge which appears to be closest to the viewer) and two *base lines*, at 30° to the horizontal.

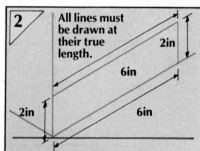

2

All lines must be drawn at their true length.

2in

6in

2in

6in

Mark the object's length and width along the base lines, and its height along the leading edge. Then construct the object's front face.

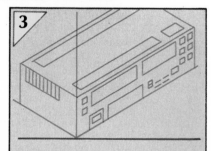

3

Draw the side and top in the same way. Horizontals are parallel to the base lines and verticals are parallel to the leading edge.

Irregular shapes

It is easier to draw objects with irregular shapes, like the chair shown on the right, if you first draw a box enclosing the object. This provides a framework to cut down on the number of *construction lines* needed, and helps position your drawing on the page. Draw the object's outline inside the box.

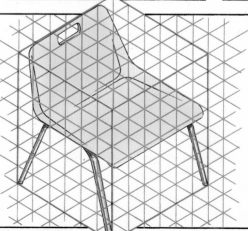

Isometric grid paper

Isometric *grid* paper is printed with vertical and 30° lines to make isometric drawing simple to do. The chair on the left is drawn on this kind of paper. You trace off the main outlines along the grid lines.

Exploded drawings

Exploded drawings show how the parts of an object fit together, by drawing them hovering in space around the object. Isometric exploded drawings are often used, as they are easier than drawing in perspective, and give true dimensions.

This simple exploded drawing shows the parts of a pencil sharpener. In isometric drawings circular parts like the hole and the screw are drawn in a special way. The steps below show you how.

---

1   **Isometric circles**

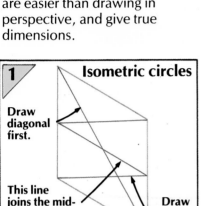

Draw diagonal first.

This line joins the mid-points of the sides.

Draw these lines last.

Draw an isometric square with sides the same length as the circle's diameter. Then draw in the lines shown in blue.

2

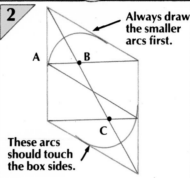

Always draw the smaller arcs first.

A   B

C

These arcs should touch the box sides.

Set your compasses to the length AB. With the point on B, draw an *arc*. With the same radius and the point on C, draw a second arc.

3

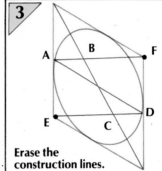

A   B   F

E   C   D

Erase the construction lines.

Set your compasses to the length ED. Put the point at E and draw an arc to touch the box sides. Draw a second arc with the point at F.

How you can use isometric drawings

An isometric drawing is an easy way to draw your own designs in three dimensions. Try drawing exciting buildings or your own inventions, like the spacecraft shown here. The steps below show how to construct a drawing like this*.

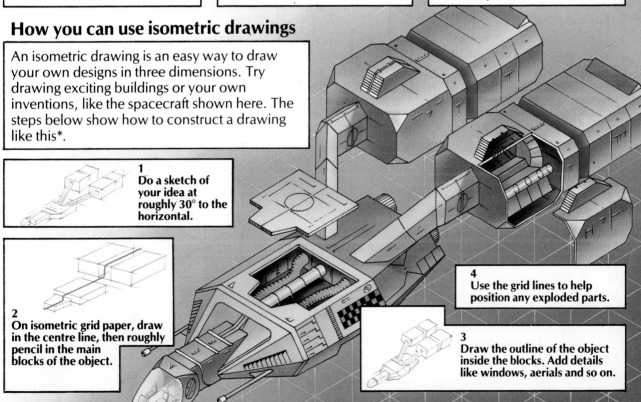

1
Do a sketch of your idea at roughly 30° to the horizontal.

2
On isometric grid paper, draw in the centre line, then roughly pencil in the main blocks of the object.

3
Draw the outline of the object inside the blocks. Add details like windows, aerials and so on.

4
Use the grid lines to help position any exploded parts.

*There are tips on how to colour drawings like this on pages 28-31.

Perspective drawing

Perspective is a method of drawing solid objects to make them look realistic. It attempts to reproduce what is seen in real life. Perspective is widely used for presentation drawings (drawings that a designer shows to a client), as it is the simplest way to show what something will actually look like.

Vanishing points

Horizon line

Vanishing point

Vanishing point

Extend these lines.

On the picture above, if you extend all the lines leading into the distance (called *receding lines*) you can see that they meet at two points. These are called *vanishing points*, and they are always situated on the *horizon*.

There are two main methods of perspective drawing: *one-point*, which has one vanishing point; and *two-point*, which has two vanishing points. You can find out more about the two methods on these pages.

Viewpoints and horizon

Horizon

The horizon is always in line with the viewer's eye level. If you are standing on flat ground, the horizon naturally falls about half-way up the scene.

Horizon

On a hill, you have a high viewpoint, so the horizon falls near the top of what you see. A high horizon makes your subject look small or far off.

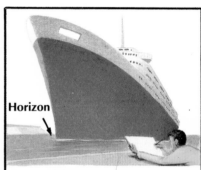

Horizon

On the ground, you have a low viewpoint, so the horizon falls near the bottom of what you see. A low horizon makes a subject look large or close up.

One-point perspective

One-point is the simplest perspective, and is used to show head-on views, such as interior views in architecture.

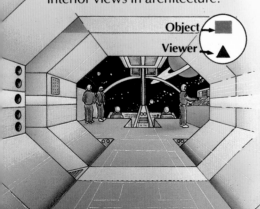

Object

Viewer

Vanishing point

1 Choose a horizon line and mark the vanishing point.

2 Mark the width of the object.

3 Draw the front view of the object.

4 Join the ends of this line to the vanishing point.

5 Construct the rest of the object between the receding lines.

6 Erase the construction lines.

Two-point perspective

Two-point perspective is used to draw objects which are at an angle to the viewer like the house on the right.

In two-point perspective there are two vanishing points: the left and the right-hand vanishing point. These are often abbreviated to VPL and VPR.

The steps below show how to construct a drawing in this type of perspective.

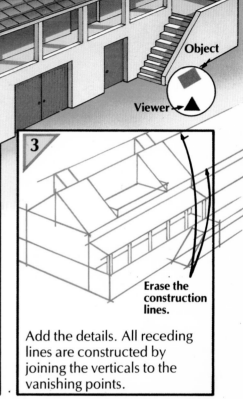

Object

Viewer

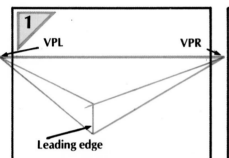

1

VPL   VPR

Leading edge

Draw the horizon line and two vanishing points, then mark in the *leading edge*. Join the ends of the leading edge to the two vanishing points.

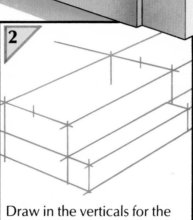

2

Draw in the verticals for the front and side views. Complete the outline by joining the ends to the opposite vanishing points.

3

Erase the construction lines.

Add the details. All receding lines are constructed by joining the verticals to the vanishing points.

Viewpoint in two-point perspective

In a two-point drawing, the viewpoint is governed by the position of the leading edge in relation to the horizon line.

Placing the leading edge below the horizon gives the impression of looking down on the subject.

If the leading edge is *bisected* by the horizon line, you appear to be viewing the subject straight on.

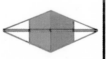

Placing the leading edge above the horizon gives the impression of looking up at the subject.

Positioning the vanishing points

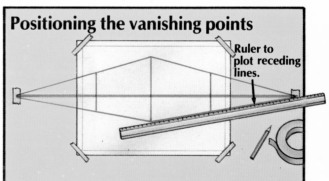

Ruler to plot receding lines.

To avoid distortion, it is best to position the vanishing points as far apart as possible. If the vanishing points are on the paper, you will end up with a small drawing in the middle and lots of blank space. You can avoid this by positioning the vanishing points on your drawing board or table and marking them with masking tape.

Using perspective

Circles in perspective

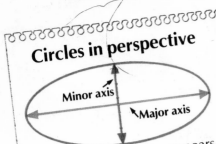

Minor axis

Major axis

A circle in *perspective* appears to be an oval shape, called an *ellipse*. An ellipse has two *axes*: the major axis along its length, and the minor axis along its width. There are several ways of drawing them, explained on this page.

Drawing ellipses freehand

It is often easiest to draw small ellipses freehand*. The motorcycle wheel on the right was first drawn in this way. Draw a box first as a framework, then sketch in the ellipse.

The ellipse touches the box at the mid-point of each side.

An ellipse always has rounded ends – not pointed ones.

---

1 Constructing an ellipse

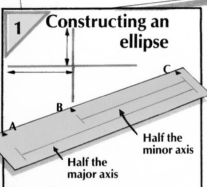

C

B

A

Half the minor axis

Half the major axis

Draw the major and minor axes, intersecting at 90°. Cut a strip of paper with a straight edge to use as a trammel**, and mark it as shown above.

2

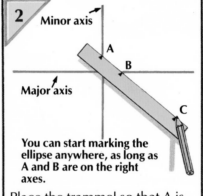

Minor axis

A

B

Major axis

C

You can start marking the ellipse anywhere, as long as A and B are on the right axes.

Place the trammel so that A is on the minor axis and B on the major axis, then mark the position of C with a pencil.

3

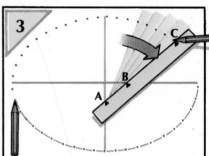

C

B

A

Gradually move the trammel around, keeping A and B on the axes. Plot the position of C as you go, as points to form an outline. Then join the points freehand.

---

1 Making an elliptical photo frame

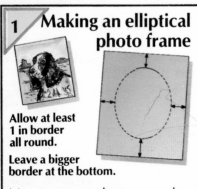

Allow at least 1 in border all round.

Leave a bigger border at the bottom.

Measure your photo to work out the size of elliptical hole needed. Cut a piece of stiff paper big enough for the ellipse and a border all round.

2

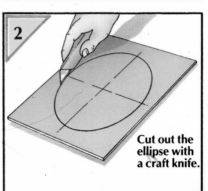

Cut out the ellipse with a craft knife.

Measure and pencil in the major and minor ellipse axes in the centre of the paper. Then draw the ellipse by the trammel method shown above.

3

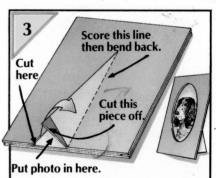

Score this line then bend back.

Cut here

Cut this piece off.

Put photo in here.

Cut a piece of card the same size as the frame. Cut a support from the card as shown above. Stick the frame to the card with glue round the top and sides.

---

*You could also use an ellipse guide – see page 39.

**The name trammel comes from a piece of drawing equipment used for drawing circles and ellipse

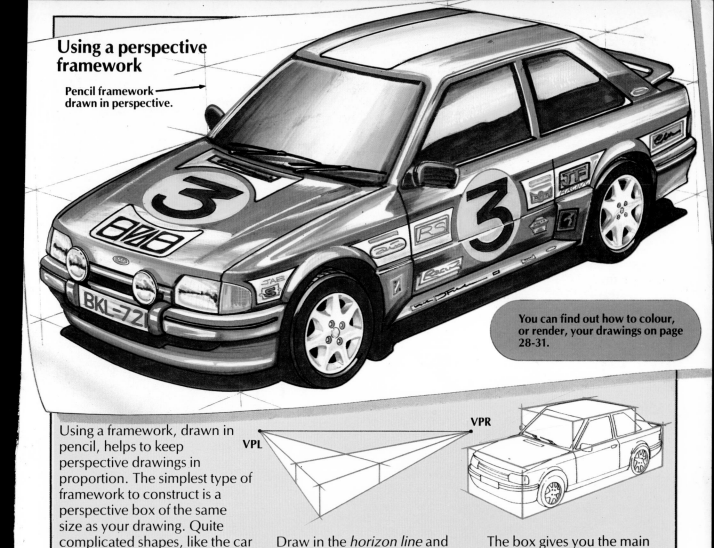

Using a perspective framework

Pencil framework drawn in perspective.

You can find out how to colour, or render, your drawings on page 28-31.

Using a framework, drawn in pencil, helps to keep perspective drawings in proportion. The simplest type of framework to construct is a perspective box of the same size as your drawing. Quite complicated shapes, like the car shown above, can be constructed in this way from a series of boxes.

Draw in the *horizon line* and two *vanishing points*, then construct a box (or boxes) in perspective (see page 25).

The box gives you the main outlines of your drawing, then you can sketch in the details freehand.

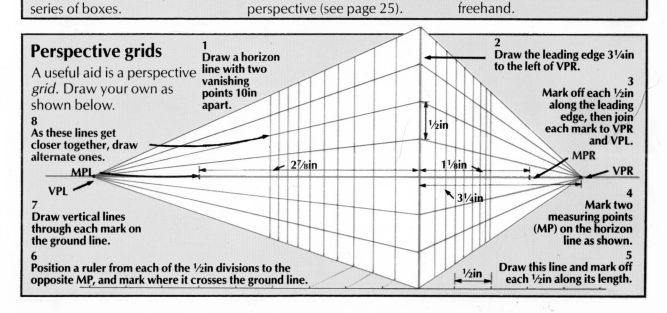

Perspective grids

A useful aid is a perspective *grid*. Draw your own as shown below.

1 Draw a horizon line with two vanishing points 10in apart.

2 Draw the leading edge 3¼in to the left of VPR.

3 Mark off each ½in along the leading edge, then join each mark to VPR and VPL.

4 Mark two measuring points (MP) on the horizon line as shown.

5 Draw this line and mark off each ½in along its length.

6 Position a ruler from each of the ½in divisions to the opposite MP, and mark where it crosses the ground line.

7 Draw vertical lines through each mark on the ground line.

8 As these lines get closer together, draw alternate ones.

Labels: VPL, MPL, VPR, MPR, ½in, 2⅞in, 1⅛in, 3¼in, ½in

Rendering techniques

Designers usually *render*, or colour, drawings that will be presented to clients, as this makes the drawings look much more exciting and realistic, and gives the impression of three dimensions.

There are lots of different rendering techniques, using pencils, pens and paints, which are explained on the next four pages. It is a good idea to practise on some rough paper before you start.

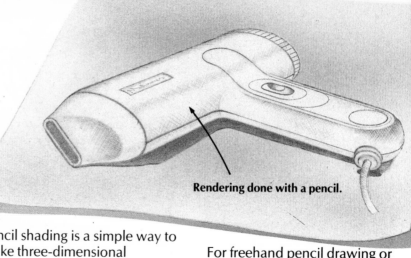

Rendering done with a pencil.

Pencil shading is a simple way to make three-dimensional drawings look convincingly realistic.

For freehand pencil drawing or shading use construction paper and a soft pencil (a B or softer).

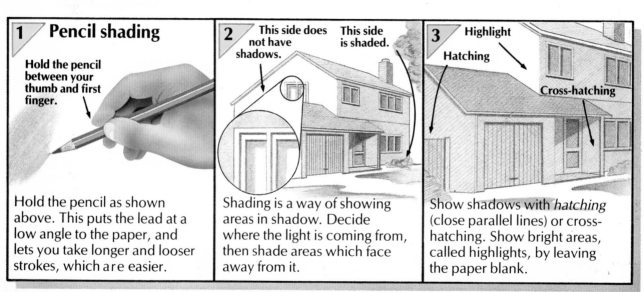

1 Pencil shading

Hold the pencil between your thumb and first finger.

Hold the pencil as shown above. This puts the lead at a low angle to the paper, and lets you take longer and looser strokes, which are easier.

2

This side does not have shadows.

This side is shaded.

Shading is a way of showing areas in shadow. Decide where the light is coming from, then shade areas which face away from it.

3

Highlight

Hatching

Cross-hatching

Show shadows with *hatching* (close parallel lines) or cross-hatching. Show bright areas, called highlights, by leaving the paper blank.

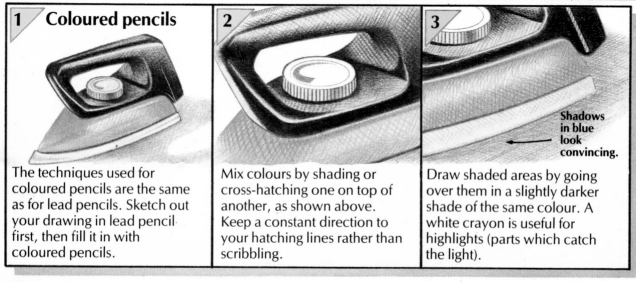

1 Coloured pencils

The techniques used for coloured pencils are the same as for lead pencils. Sketch out your drawing in lead pencil first, then fill it in with coloured pencils.

2

Mix colours by shading or cross-hatching one on top of another, as shown above. Keep a constant direction to your hatching lines rather than scribbling.

3

Shadows in blue look convincing.

Draw shaded areas by going over them in a slightly darker shade of the same colour. A white crayon is useful for highlights (parts which catch the light).

Marker pens

Markers are thick felt pens which are ideal for quick sketches, big illustrations and filling in large blocks of colour. Because they are so thick, markers are not suitable for small or detailed work. Fibre tip pens are best for finer work.

Markers are quite expensive, so it is best to buy just a few at first, such as the primary colours (red, blue and yellow), grey and black. Always recap your markers after use to prevent them drying out.

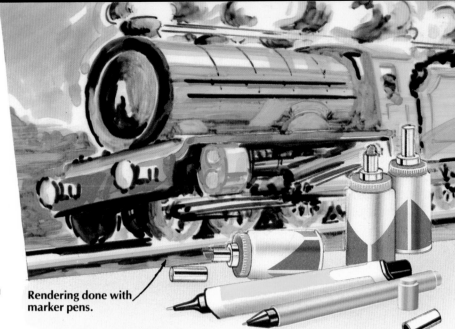

Rendering done with marker pens.

Choosing paper

Glue to stick tracing paper to white paper.

Mount tracing paper on white paper to show up the colours.

Markers bleed on ordinary paper. This spoils outlines and stains the lower sheets of a pad. Tracing paper or special bleedproof marker paper are best, as they do not let the colour soak through.

Using the tip

1

Use the narrowest edge for drawing and outlining.

2

Use the widest surface for colouring in large areas.

Markers have a chisel tip, which gives different line thicknesses according to how you hold the pen (see above). To get an even tone, it is best to colour quickly from side to side. Keep the marker tip moving all the time to stop it blotting.

Darker tones

Make sure each layer is dry before you colour over it.

You can get different *tones* (shades of one colour) from a marker by colouring an area two or three times. This technique is useful for showing areas in shadow. Darker areas can also be made by going over the original colour in light grey.

Masking

Test the tape first to make sure it does not damage the surface of your paper.

Tidy up uneven edges with a coloured pencil.

Masking tape is useful if you want to make a straight edge. Stick tape along the edge, then colour from side to side across the tape, not along it. Peel the tape away when the ink is dry. Colour may bleed slightly under the tape.

More rendering techniques

Watercolours

Watercolour paints are used to *render* presentation drawings and as washes (watery layers of paint), to make parts of a drawing stand out. Washes are often used in architectural drawing.

Construction paper is best for watercolour rendering. Stretch it* first, otherwise it will cockle when it gets damp.

Washes

Start a wash at the top of the drawing and work downwards. Fill your brush and use long horizontal brush strokes to bring the wash down the drawing. Use a damp brush to remove any excess wash.

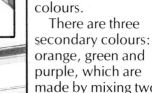

Stick masking tape round the paintbrush handle to give a better grip.

Use the brush to draw the wash along.

Draw the bristles to a point for a thin line.

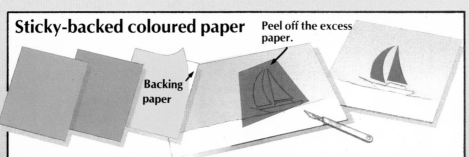

Make darker tones by laying one wash of colour over another. Leave the colour to dry before painting on top.

The best watercolour brushes are made of sable and are expensive, but you can get good nylon brushes which are much cheaper.

Paint round the edges with a thin brush first, then fill in the rest of the shape with a larger brush.

Mix colours with a wet brush in the lid of your paint box or on a palette. Never mix colours on the picture.

Colour and tone

There are three primary colours: red, yellow and blue. These can not be made from other colours, but they can be mixed together to create all other colours.

There are three secondary colours: orange, green and purple, which are made by mixing two primary colours.

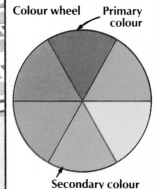

Colour wheel

Primary colour

Secondary colour

Each secondary is a mixture of the primaries on either side.

Complementary colours

Colours opposite each other on the colour wheel are called complementary colours. Placing complementary colours together gives a very vivid effect.

Tone

The lightness or darkness of a colour is called its tone. Black and white photos show tone well as all colours are reduced to different tones of grey.

Sticky-backed coloured paper

Peel off the excess paper.

Backing paper

You can buy special sticky-backed coloured paper and film in art shops. It is useful for filling in large areas of flat colour on models or drawings.

Draw the outline, then cut a piece of paper big enough to cover the shape. Peel off the backing and stick the paper down. Trim with an Exacto-knife.

You can create different tones and colours by sticking one piece of paper on top of another. Draw details on top of the paper.

You can find out how to stretch paper on page 35.

Airbrush

An airbrush is a device for spraying paint. A simple modeller's airbrush is useful for filling in large areas of colour and painting models. An artist's airbrush is expensive, but does very detailed work*.

You also need a compressed air supply, called a propellant. You can get aerosol cans of propellant or a mains electricity air compressor. Only buy one if you do a lot of airbrushing.

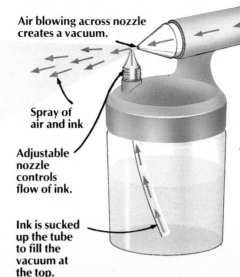

Air blowing across nozzle creates a vacuum.

Valve for switching air on and off.

Spray of air and ink

An airbrush can spray any kind of liquid paint or ink.

Adjustable nozzle controls flow of ink.

Tube to propellant

Ink is sucked up the tube to fill the vacuum at the top.

An airbrush sprays air and ink to produce a flat and even colour. On an artist's airbrush the air supply valve can also control the amount of air flowing through the nozzle, making it possible to do detailed work.

Using an airbrush

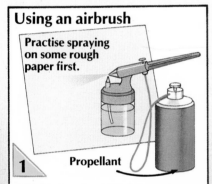

Practise spraying on some rough paper first.

1

Propellant

Fill the bottle with ink and connect the air tube to the propellant. Practise spraying and adjust the nozzle until the ink flows evenly.

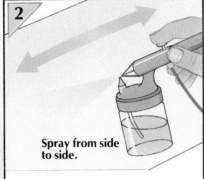

2

Spray from side to side.

For large areas, keep the airbrush moving all the time so the colour is even. Do not spray close to the paper or the ink will form a puddle.

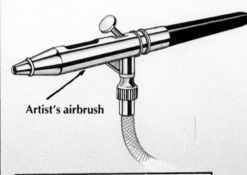

Artist's airbrush

Cleaning an airbrush

It is important to clean an airbrush each time you change inks as well as after using it. Any dried ink or grit in the tubes will prevent it spraying evenly.

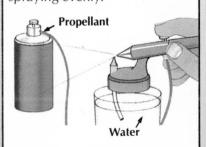

Propellant

Water

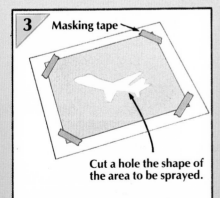

3

Masking tape

Cut a hole the shape of the area to be sprayed.

You need a mask to get a neat outline. Cut one from paper or card** to cover areas you do not want to colour.

4

This is called overspray.

Spray from side to side across the paper over the edges of the mask. Wait until the paint is dry, then remove the mask.

Empty the ink container and spray any remaining ink on to scrap paper. Fill the ink container with water, then spray this through the tubes to clean them out.

Most of the illustrations in this book were done with an airbrush.
**You can get special masking film which peels off without damaging your drawing.*

Using photographs

Photographs are useful as reminders of what an object looks like (called reference material), to trace from and as backgrounds for your own drawings. Any kind of camera is useful, but those with close-up focus are best. Pictures from magazines can be used instead of specially-taken photographs, so your own camera is not essential.

Taking your own reference photos

If you are taking your own reference pictures, a black and white film is often best as the pictures are often clearer and sharper than colour. Take lots of photos from different viewpoints, as this will help you to decide which is the most suitable view for the final drawing.

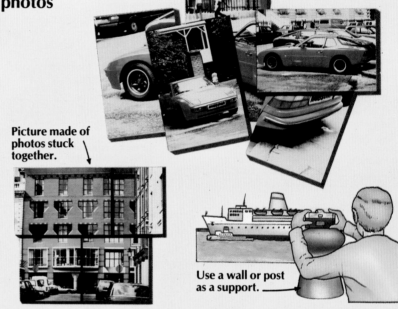

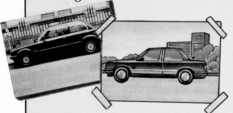

Picture made of photos stuck together.

Use a wall or post as a support.

Side and *front* views are useful, as these show true lengths and can be used to *dimension* your drawing. Dividers are useful for comparing proportions on the photo and the drawing.

The details in a photograph taken from a long way off will be blurred. To avoid this, take several overlapping photos, as close to the object as you can get, and stick them together as shown.

To take a series of overlapping photos, support the camera on something, so that the viewpoint will be the same in all the pictures. You could use a wall or post.

Photos as background

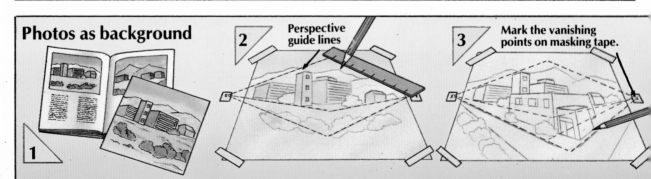

2 Perspective guide lines

3 Mark the vanishing points on masking tape.

1 Take a background photo or use a picture from a magazine. You can enlarge these to a suitable size on a photocopier*.

Place tracing paper over the photo. Draw in the *receding lines* of buildings or objects in the photo. Project the *vanishing points* from these lines.

Using the *perspective* guide lines, do your drawing on the tracing paper. Trace this on to drawing paper, cut it out and glue it to the photo.

Tracing from a photograph

Tracing from a photograph or a picture is an easy way to get an accurate outline of an object without setting up the perspective yourself. The steps below show you how.

You can either ink in the outline with a technical pen, or render it in colour. Inking in is a good way to practise using technical pens, which are often used to outline engineering and architectural drawings.

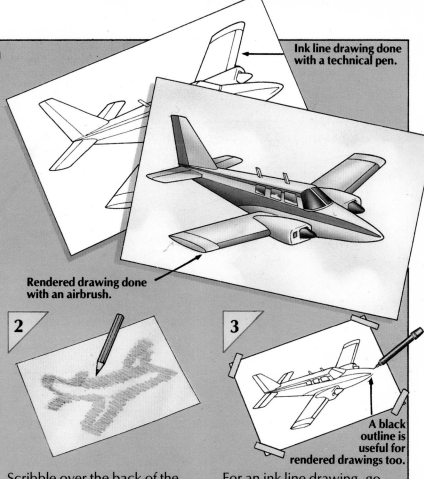

Ink line drawing done with a technical pen.

Rendered drawing done with an airbrush.

1 Use a sharp 2H pencil.

Photo

Tracing paper

Trace over the outline of the object. Omit unnecessary details, shadows or reflections. Try to keep a steady hand so the lines will be straight.

2

Scribble over the back of the tracing with a soft pencil. Put the tracing over your drawing paper, and go over the outline again, this time with a 2H pencil.

3

A black outline is useful for rendered drawings too.

For an ink line drawing, go over the outline with a technical pen or thin felt pen. You could also use the tracing as an outline for a rendered drawing.

4

Render your drawing. If using a photocopied background render this too. Don't use marker pens, as they contain solvent which smudges photocopies.

Photographs vs drawings

*A photo is not usually focused all over, and some parts can be quite blurred. In a drawing the focus is sharp all over.

*In a photo you get a lot of objects in the background which you may not want. In a drawing you can choose your own background.

*Some camera lenses distort the shape of objects, especially near the edge of the picture.

No unwanted background.

Drawings can show how an object works.

*A photo can only show the object as it actually is, whereas a drawing can depict the object for a particular purpose, such as to show how it works.

Finishing touches

People react favourably to well-presented drawings. Using mounts and frames makes your drawings look professional and need not cost much, as you can make them yourself from paper or card.

There are some useful tips on these pages to help you present your drawings in a neat and professional way, both for exhibitions and for keeping them yourself.

Mounting drawings

A mount is a piece of card used to display a drawing. The simplest way to mount a drawing is to stick it to a thick paper or card backing, using one of the glues described on this page.

It is a good idea to cut out a damaged or dirtied drawing, and stick it to a fresh sheet of paper before mounting. Use an Exacto-knife to trim carefully round the outline.

Glue

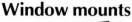

Never use spray glue in an enclosed space – it can damage your lungs if inhaled.

Scrap paper to stop glue getting on table.

Several types of glue are suitable for mounting. The easiest to use is spray glue. Glues which do not bond on contact are good as you can reposition anything crooked.

Rubber cement

Rubber cement sticks on contact, so you cannot adjust things.

Spread the glue thinly and evenly over both surfaces with a spatula or piece of card. Leave the glue for a few minutes to dry, then stick the surfaces together.

Double-sided tape

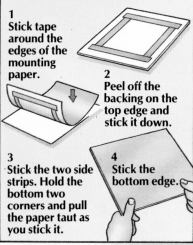

1 Stick tape around the edges of the mounting paper.

2 Peel off the backing on the top edge and stick it down.

3 Stick the two side strips. Hold the bottom two corners and pull the paper taut as you stick it.

4 Stick the bottom edge.

Window mounts

A window mount is a piece of paper or card with a "window" cut in it to make a frame. It is glued to the edges of a drawing.

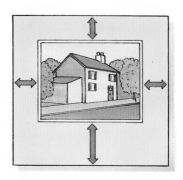

A window mount can be any shape, but it looks best if the frame is the same width at the sides and top, and wider at the bottom.

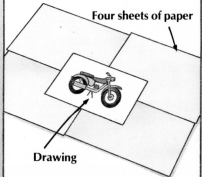

Four sheets of paper

Drawing

Adjust paper to the right size.

Work out the size of your mount with some rough paper as shown above. Then take measurements to transfer to the card.

Protecting drawings

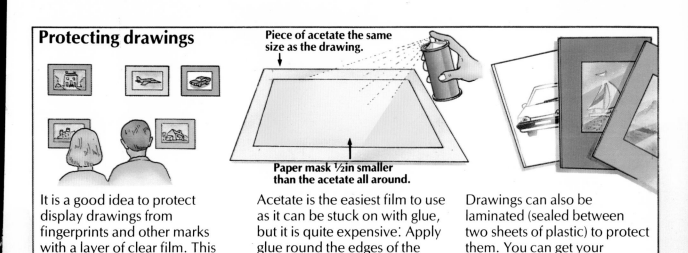

Piece of acetate the same size as the drawing.

Paper mask ½in smaller than the acetate all around.

It is a good idea to protect display drawings from fingerprints and other marks with a layer of clear film. This also makes your drawings look professional.

Acetate is the easiest film to use as it can be stuck on with glue, but it is quite expensive: Apply glue round the edges of the acetate as shown above by masking with a piece of paper.

Drawings can also be laminated (sealed between two sheets of plastic) to protect them. You can get your drawings laminated at an instant print shop.

Stretching paper

Drawings *rendered* in watercolour work best on stretched construction paper. This prevents the paper cockling (wrinkling) as the paint dries.

1

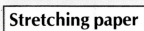

Immerse the paper in a bowl of clean water. Shake the drips off, and place the paper flat on a wooden drawing board.

2

Stick the paper to the board with gummed brown paper tape round all the edges. Mop off excess water with a sponge.

3

Cut the paper off with an Exacto-knife when your painting is finished and dry.

Keeping a portfolio

A portfolio is useful to protect your drawings. You can buy them from art or graphics shops, but they can be expensive. The steps below will show you how to make your own from card.

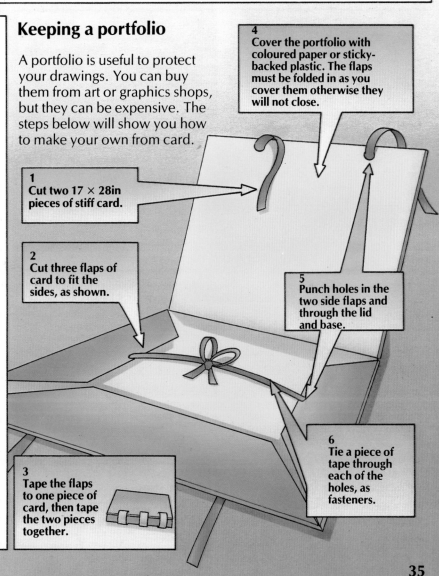

1
Cut two 17 × 28in pieces of stiff card.

2
Cut three flaps of card to fit the sides, as shown.

3
Tape the flaps to one piece of card, then tape the two pieces together.

4
Cover the portfolio with coloured paper or sticky-backed plastic. The flaps must be folded in as you cover them otherwise they will not close.

5
Punch holes in the two side flaps and through the lid and base.

6
Tie a piece of tape through each of the holes, as fasteners.

How a professional designer works

Technical drawings and models are a vital stage in the design of new products, such as cars, washing machines and radios. They help to decide many things about the product, such as its final size and shape.

Here you can find out how a design team helps to develop a new car. The same principles apply to the design of any new product.

The research stage

Before the design team set to work the company does some market research. They ask customers questions to see what kind of car there is a demand for.

The company's engineers provide technical information on the materials to be used, the equipment available for building the car and aerodynamic shapes.

The design stages

1
The design team are given a brief (some instructions) made up of the market research ideas and the engineering specifications.

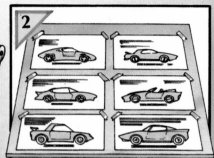

2
First the design team do a series of sketches to experiment with different ideas to show what the car might look like, both inside and outside.

3
Marker pens are often used for rendering cars.

Next they produce *rendered perspective* drawings of the most successful sketches. These are presented to the head designers, who decide which ideas are best.

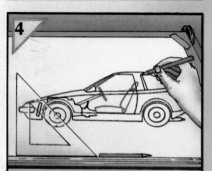

4
Before a model is made, a designer does an *orthographic projection*. This gives more precise information about the car's size and shape.

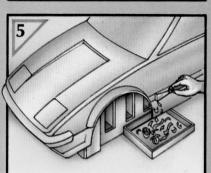

5
Next the ideas are presented to the company's managers, and one design is selected. The team then make a full-size clay model of the selected car design.

6
If the clay model is unsatisfactory, the design team make more sketches and models until everyone is happy with the design.

7

Computer-controlled
measuring machine

A computer-controlled machine takes measurements from the final clay model. These are stored in the computer and are later used to make the car parts.

8

Next a full-size glass fibre model of the chosen design is made. The market research department shows this to customers to see if they like the car.

9

Light pen

Engineers call up diagrams of parts of the car on a computer terminal and make any minor adjustments with a light pen. This is called *CAD – computer-aided design*

10

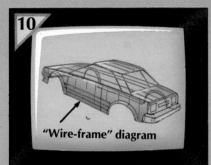

"Wire-frame" diagram

When all the parts are designed, the complete body structure can be seen on the computer terminal as a "wire-frame" diagram.

11

Designers use the "wire-frame" diagram to test for stress points and how the car would react in a crash. The design is then modified if necessary.

12

A prototype car is built from the information in the computer. It is tested for safety, durability, noise levels, rusting and extreme weather conditions.

Making the car

When the prototype has been adjusted to pass all the tests, production of the actual car can start.

Technical drawing equipment

On these pages there is a list of all the basic materials and equipment mentioned in this book, together with suggestions about more advanced equipment to buy if you have a little more money to spend.

You can also read about the different paper sizes that are available and the range of pencil hardnesses to choose from.

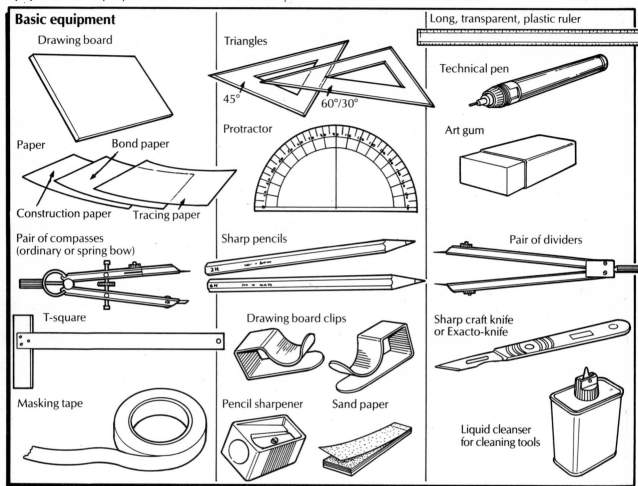

Basic equipment

Drawing board

Triangles

45° 60°/30°

Long, transparent, plastic ruler

Technical pen

Paper Bond paper

Construction paper Tracing paper

Protractor

Art gum

Pair of compasses (ordinary or spring bow)

Sharp pencils

Pair of dividers

T-square

Drawing board clips

Sharp craft knife or Exacto-knife

Masking tape

Pencil sharpener Sand paper

Liquid cleanser for cleaning tools

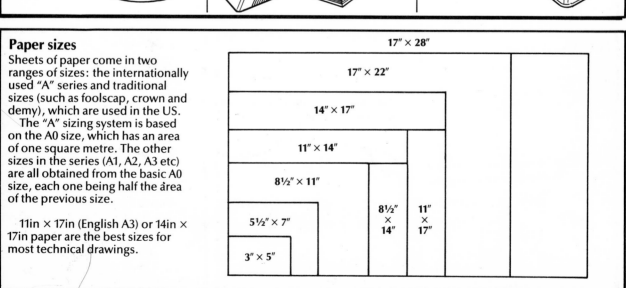

Paper sizes

Sheets of paper come in two ranges of sizes: the internationally used "A" series and traditional sizes (such as foolscap, crown and demy), which are used in the US.

The "A" sizing system is based on the A0 size, which has an area of one square metre. The other sizes in the series (A1, A2, A3 etc) are all obtained from the basic A0 size, each one being half the area of the previous size.

11in × 17in (English A3) or 14in × 17in paper are the best sizes for most technical drawings.

17" × 28"

17" × 22"

14" × 17"

11" × 14"

8½" × 11"

5½" × 7"

8½" × 14"

11" × 17"

3" × 5"

Advanced equipment

 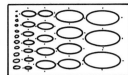

Ellipse and circle guides: templates for drawing *ellipses* and circles.

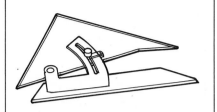

Adjustable triangle: this can be adjusted to measure any angle between 45° and 90°.

French curves: used to draw curved lines.

Parallel motion drawing board; this has a fitted T-square which moves up and down on a pulley system.

Scale rules: these are used when drawing to *scale*. They are divided up according to the most commonly used scales.

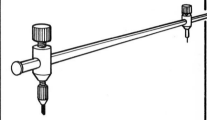

Beam compass: a special compass for drawing large circles. The pencil fitting is screwed to a horizontal bar to give a large radius.

Ruling pen: an adjustable ink pen used to draw lines of different thickness. These are difficult to use – technical pens are easier.

Flexible curves: lengths of pliable plastic which can be bent to any curve.

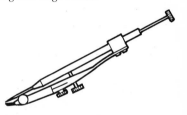

Drop compass: a compass for drawing very small circles.

Pencil hardnesses

Pencils are graded according to their hardness, from 9H to 7B. H stands for hard, and B stands for black. The pencil "lead" is actually made from a mixture of graphite (which makes the marks) and clay (which binds the graphite together). The more clay there is in the lead, the harder the pencil is.

The table below shows the range of pencils and what they are used for.

9H-5H: Extra hard – special pencils used for draughting.

4H and 3H: Very hard – used for *construction*, *dimension* and *projection lines*.

2H and H: Hard – used for *outlines* on technical drawings.

HB, B and 2B: Soft – used for freehand drawing and sketching.

3B-7B: Very soft – for shading.

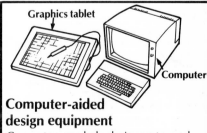

Graphics tablet

Computer

Computer-aided design equipment

Computers can help designers to work much faster than drawing with conventional equipment. This is called *computer-aided design* (CAD).

The designer uses a graphics tablet (an electronic drawing board linked to the computer), or a light pen, which can "draw" straight on to the screen. The computer stores the dimensions and can print out the drawing.

Geometry tips

Geometry is often used in technical drawing, to do things like dividing angles and lines in half. Below are some simple geometrical methods which you will often need to use in your drawings.

Bisecting an angle

Bisect means divide in half.

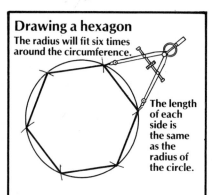

This radius can be any length.

Put a compass point on A and mark off the *arcs* at B and C. Then put the compass point on B and C in turn and draw the two intersecting arcs at D. The line from A to D *bisects* the angle.

Bisecting a line

Set your compasses to more than half the length of the line to be bisected. Put the compass point at A and B in turn and mark the arcs at C and D. The line from C to D bisects AB.

Rounded corners

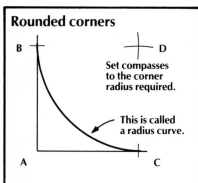

Set compasses to the corner radius required.

This is called a radius curve.

With the compass point at A, draw the arcs at B and C. Put the compass point at B and C in turn and draw the intersecting arcs at D. Then at D to draw an arc to touch the corner lines at B and C.

Drawing a hexagon

The radius will fit six times around the circumference.

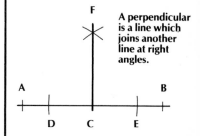

The length of each side is the same as the radius of the circle.

Draw a circle and with the same radius mark off arcs around the circumference as shown above. With a ruler join the six arcs to form a hexagon.

Drawing a perpendicular

A perpendicular is a line which joins another line at right angles.

Set your compasses to a radius less than A to C. Put the point on C and mark the arcs at D and E. Then with a larger radius and the point on D and E in turn, mark the arcs at F. The line F to C is *perpendicular* to AB.

Things to draw

These optical illusions are easy to draw and good practice to get used to using your equipment. The steps below will show you how to draw them.

The horizontal lines are all ▶ parallel, although they do not look it. Draw them first, using a T-square. The sloping lines are at 30° to the horizontal – use a 60°/30° triangle.

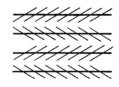

The two black circles are the ▶ same size, although one appears larger than the other. Draw the black circles first, with the same radius, then add the surrounding circles.

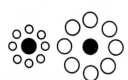

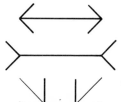

◀ The two horizontal lines are the same length, although one looks longer. Draw them first with a T-square and triangle. Draw the arrows with a 45° triangle.

◀ The two vertical lines are parallel, although they look curved. Mark off 15° divisions with a protractor, then draw in the radiating lines. Draw the two vertical lines either side of the centre.

Studio tips

Using tracing paper

If a drawing does not look right first time, do not throw it away. Trace the *layout* or the good parts on to fresh paper to save having to start the whole drawing from scratch.

Bevelled instruments

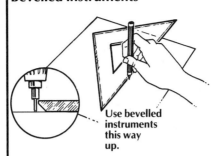

Use bevelled instruments this way up.

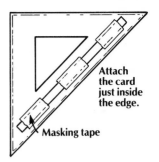

Attach the card just inside the edge.

Masking tape

A *bevel* is a sloping edge on drawing instruments which makes it easier to ink lines. It prevents smudging as it keeps the instruments away from the ink link. There are bevels on rulers, triangles and protractors.

If your equipment does not have bevelled edges, you can get the same effect by sticking on a strip of card, as shown above. Attach the card securely with masking tape or double-sided tape.

Inking in lines

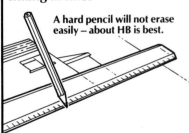

A hard pencil will not erase easily – about HB is best.

Art gum is best as it will not remove any ink.

It is best to mark out guidelines in pencil first to show where the ink lines will go. Keep your lines very faint, and draw as little as possible – points or dashes are often enough to indicate the position of a line.

Ink over the lines with a technical pen. If the ink does not flow evenly, shake the pen from side to side horizontally. Leave the ink to dry thoroughly before you erase any pencil *construction lines* that show through.

Drying drawings

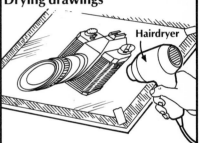

Hairdryer

A hairdryer is useful for drying ink and paint drawings quickly. Keep the hairdryer nozzle well away from your drawing, otherwise you may cockle the paper or blow the wet ink around.

Keeping drawings clean

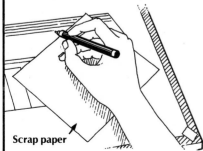

Scrap paper

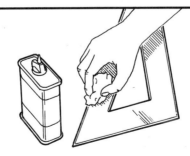

Cover paper

Stick paper to the back of the drawing.

Drawings look best if kept clean and smudge-free. Always wash your hands before starting and if you get any paint on them. Some scrap paper under your hand will stop you marking the drawing paper.

Tissue paper soaked in liquid cleanser is useful for cleaning ink and other marks from your equipment. It will also remove greasy marks from drawings, but test your paper first to make sure it does not stain.

Always protect your unfinished drawings from dust and other marks. Either keep them in a portfolio*, or cover them with a sheet of paper, as shown above.

*You can find out how to make your own portfolio on page 35.

Drawing conventions

A *convention* is a standard way of representing features on technical drawings. On these pages you can find out about some of the conventions and about different ways of showing *dimensions* and sections on drawings. There is also a list of common abbreviations, and information about when to use different kinds of lines on your drawings.

Abbreviations

Abbreviation	Meaning	Symbol
A/F	Across flats	
C, CL or c	Centre line	
CH HD	Cheese head	
CAD	Computer-aided design	
CSK HD	Countersunk head	

Abbreviation	Meaning
DIA / Ø	Diameter: in a note / before a dimension
DRG	Drawing
EXT	External
HEX HD	Hexagonal head
I/D	Inside diameter
INT	Internal

Abbreviation	Meaning
ISO	International standards organization
LH	Left hand
MAX	Maximum
MPL MPR	Measuring point left/right
MIN	Minimum
NTS	Not to scale
O/D	Outside diameter

Abbreviation	Meaning
RAD / R	Radius: in a note / before a dimension
:	Ratio
RH	Right hand
SK	Sketch
SWG	Standard wire gauge
VP VPL VPR	Vanishing point / Left-hand / Right-hand

Dimensioning

Dimensions have to be clearly shown on technical drawings. The usual way of doing this is to draw dimension lines (see page 17) and to write the dimension above the middle of the line. Below you can find out about special methods used to dimension circles, radius curves and angles.

Radius curves

Small spaces or lengths

Angles

Circles

Datum dimensioning

To show a number of dimensions along one line, (as above), measure all the lengths from one end (called the datum line), as this reduces the chance of errors building up. Each of the dimensions shows the distance from the datum line to that point.

The datum line is marked with a filled-in dot.

Lines used in technical drawing

The table below shows the main lines used in technical drawing, and where you use them.

Line	Use
————	Thick continuous line – *outlines* and edges.
————	Thin, faint continuous line – *construction*, *projection* and *dimension lines*, *hatching* and *sectioning*.
– – – –	Even dashes – *hidden details* and edges.
— · — · —	Long *chain line* – *centre lines*.
↓— · —↓	Chain line with bold ends – cutting planes.
— · — · —	Short chain line – positions of movable parts.
∿∿∿	Continuous wavy line – irregular boundary lines and short break lines.
—⟋\/⟍—	Ruled line with zigzags – long break lines.

Architectural conventions

Below you can find out the conventional methods of representing features on architectural drawings.

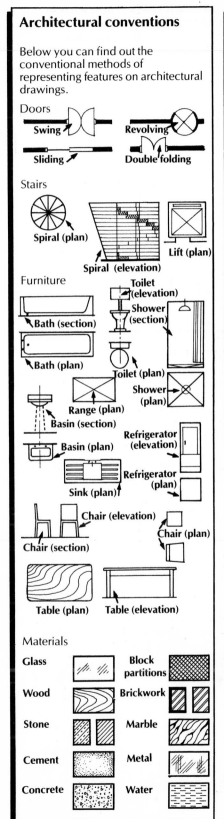

Doors

Swing

Revolving

Sliding

Double folding

Stairs

Spiral (plan)

Spiral (elevation)

Lift (plan)

Furniture

Toilet (elevation)

Shower (section)

Bath (section)

Bath (plan)

Toilet (plan)

Shower (plan)

Range (plan)

Basin (section)

Basin (plan)

Refrigerator (elevation)

Refrigerator (plan)

Sink (plan)

Chair (elevation)

Chair (plan)

Chair (section)

Table (plan)

Table (elevation)

Materials

Glass		Block partitions	
Wood		Brickwork	
Stone		Marble	
Cement		Metal	
Concrete		Water	

Engineering conventions

The drawings below show the conventional ways of representing standard features on engineering drawings.

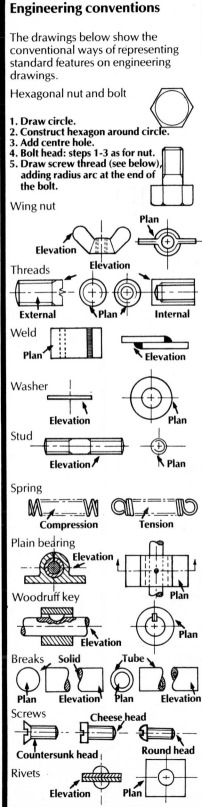

Hexagonal nut and bolt

1. Draw circle.
2. Construct hexagon around circle.
3. Add centre hole.
4. Bolt head: steps 1-3 as for nut.
5. Draw screw thread (see below), adding radius arc at the end of the bolt.

Wing nut

Plan

Elevation

Threads

Elevation

External

Plan

Internal

Weld

Plan

Elevation

Washer

Elevation

Plan

Stud

Elevation

Plan

Spring

Compression

Tension

Plain bearing

Elevation

Plan

Woodruff key

Elevation

Plan

Breaks

Solid

Tube

Plan

Elevation

Plan

Elevation

Screws

Cheese head

Countersunk head

Round head

Rivets

Elevation

Plan

Sections

A section is a view of an object cut open along a marked line to show internal details. There are different types of section, which are described below. You may need several sections to show an object fully, just as you need more than one elevation.

If you cut an object horizontally, you get a horizontal or plan section.

Cutting line

Section

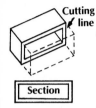

Cutting line

Section

If you cut an object vertically along its length, you get a longitudinal section.

If you cut an object vertically across its width, you get a cross section.

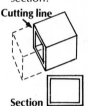

Cutting line

Section

Revolved sections

These are sections which are rotated (usually by 90°) so that you can see more of the object on the section.

Removed sections

Sections are normally projected from their original elevation. Removed sections are those which are positioned elsewhere on the drawing. They can be drawn to a larger scale, which makes dimensioning easier.

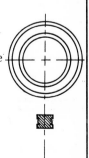

Half sections

These are drawings which show half the object as an outside view and half of it as a section.

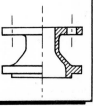

Model plans

These plans are for the models on pages 10 and 11. Either copy the plans at the same size by photocopying or tracing them, or enlarge them by following the instructions on page 46.

Draw and cut out each piece once. The solid black lines around the outside of each piece show where to cut. The dotted lines show where to make folds.

House

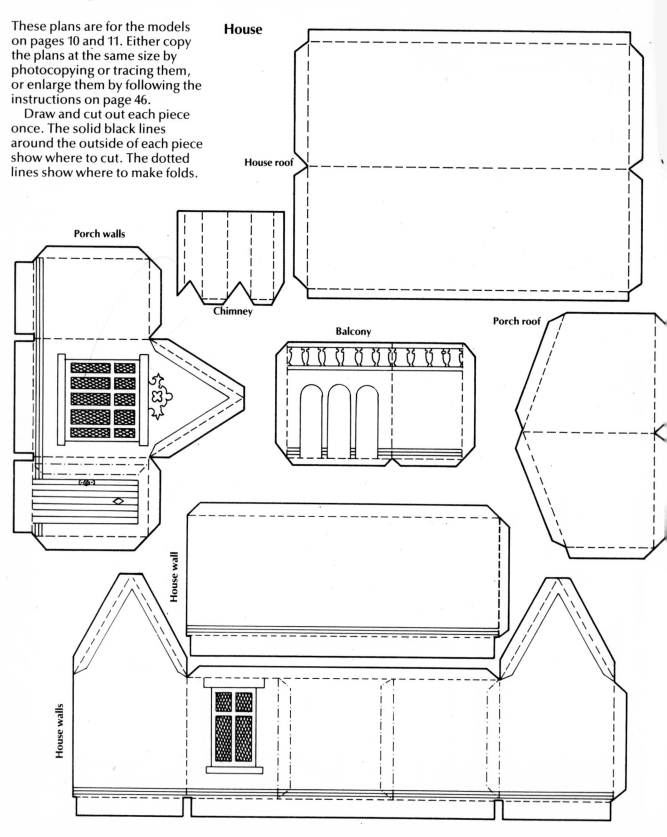

Porch walls

Chimney

House roof

Balcony

Porch roof

House wall

House walls

Truck

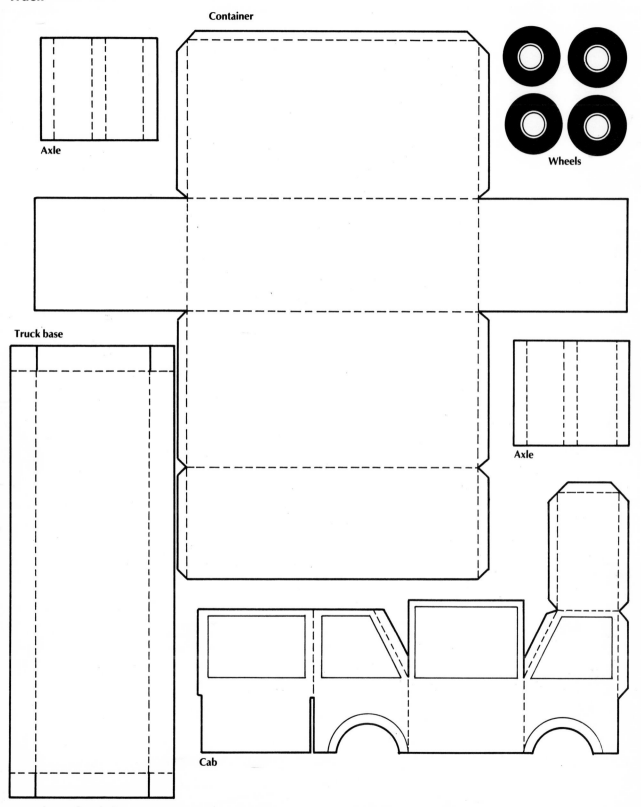

Container

Axle

Wheels

Truck base

Axle

Cab

Enlarging plans and other useful information

The tips below show how to enlarge or reduce drawings and plans using a grid. You can use this method to enlarge the plans for the model house and truck on page 44/45.

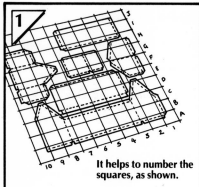

1

It helps to number the squares, as shown.

With a T-square and a triangle, draw a light pencil grid over the plans, using ½in or 1in squares. Decide how much you want to enlarge the plans – to two or three times their original size, for example.

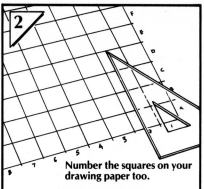

2

Number the squares on your drawing paper too.

Using a T-square and triangle, divide your drawing paper into the same number of squares. If the drawing is to be twice as big, draw squares twice the size of those on the plans, and so on.

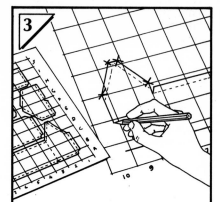

3

Copy what is in each square on the plan into the corresponding square on the paper. It is easiest to plot the points where the outlines cross the grid lines, and then join these points.

Going further

If you want to find out more about technical drawing and illustration, the books below may be useful.

For engineering drawing:

Engineering Drawing and Construction
by L.C. Mott
Oxford University Press, 1965.

Geometrical and Technical Drawing
by A. Yarwood
Nelson, 1983.

For architectural drawing:

Draughtsmanship
by Fraser Reekie
Edward Arnold, 1976.

Manual of Graphic Techniques
by Tom Porter and Sue Goodman
Astragal Books, 1985.

For perspective drawing:

Basic Perspective
by Robert W. Gill
Thames and Hudson, 1974.

For technical illustration:

Studio Tips and **More Studio Tips**
by Bill Gray
Van Nostrand Reinhold, 1976 and 1979.

Presentation Techniques
by Dick Powell
Orbis, 1985.

Answers to puzzles

Page 19

1. Plan view of a cassette tape.
2. Plan view of an aerosol can.
3. Side view of an alarm clock.
4. Plan view of a door handle
5. Plan view of a tap.
6. Side view of a ball point pen

Page 21

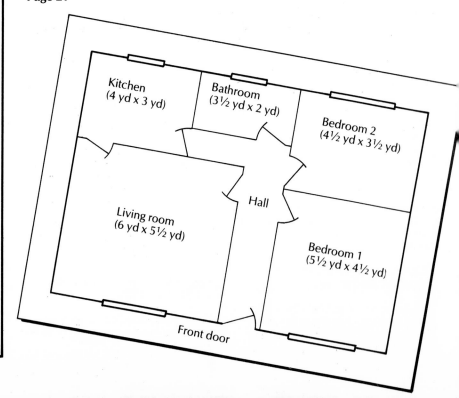

Kitchen (4 yd x 3 yd)

Bathroom (3½ yd x 2 yd)

Bedroom 2 (4½ yd x 3½ yd)

Hall

Living room (6 yd x 5½ yd)

Bedroom 1 (5½ yd x 4½ yd)

Front door

Glossary

Arc. Part of a circle's circumference.

Axis. An imaginary line through the centre of an object. For example, a line showing the length (major axis) or width (minor axis) of an *ellipse*.

Base line. A line at 30° to the horizontal, used for constructing *isometric* drawings.

Bevel. A sloping edge used on drawing instruments.

Bisect. To divide in half.

Centre lines. Thin *chain lines* used to mark the centre of circles, *arcs* and circular or *elliptical* parts.

Chain line. A line made up of alternate long and short dashes.

Computer-aided design (CAD). A computer system used in design.

Construction lines. Faint lines used to plot out basic shapes before drawing an *outline*.

Convention. A standard, internationally accepted method of representing something.

Design process. The stages a designer goes through to get from an initial idea to a finished product.

Development. A drawing showing all the surfaces of an object opened out on to one *plane*.

Dimensions. Measurements such as length and width. Dimension lines are used on drawings to show these measurements.

Elevation. In architecture, a two-dimensional drawing of the front or side of a building. In engineering, *front* and *side* views can also be called elevations.

Ellipse. An oval shape, or a circle viewed in *perspective*.

Exploded drawing. One which shows how the parts of an object fit together by showing them in space around the main piece.

First angle. Type of *orthographic projection* in which the left-hand *side view* is shown projected to the right of the *front view*, under which is the *plan view*.

Front view. Two-dimensional drawing of the front of an object, used in *orthographic projection*.

Grid. A framework of guide lines.

Hatching. Close parallel lines used for shading drawings.

Hidden details. Parts of an object which cannot be directly seen in a technical drawing. Their position is indicated by dashed lines.

Horizon line. The line where the sky appears to meet the earth. It is always at the viewer's eye level.

Isometric projection. A type of three-dimensional technical drawing in which *receding lines* are drawn at 30° to the horizontal.

Landscape. A rectangular piece of paper with the longer sides placed horizontally.

Layout. The arrangement of a drawing on the paper.

Leading edge. The vertical line which appears to be nearest the viewer in an *isometric or perspective* drawing.

Mock-up. A model.

One-point. Type of *perspective* drawing in which there is only one *vanishing point.*

Orthographic projection. Method of depicting an object by drawing a series of flat views of its different sides, arranged in a special layout.

Outline. A line showing the edges of the shape being drawn. Outlines are drawn with a continuous pencil line.

Perpendicular. A line which joins another line at 90%.

Perspective. Way of drawing solid objects to give an impression of depth and distance.

Plan view. Two-dimensional drawing of the top of an object, used in *orthographic projection*.

Plane. A flat surface.

Portrait. A rectangular piece of paper with the shorter sides placed horizontally.

Presentation drawing. One which a designer does to show a client what the design will look like.

Projection lines. Lines used in technical drawing to position *dimension lines* outside the main *outline*.

Quadrant. A quarter of a sphere or of a circle.

Ratio. A mathematical way of showing the proportion of one quantity to another, e.g. 2:1, means the drawing is twice as big as the original.

Receding lines. Lines in *perspective* and *isometric* drawings which appear to lead into the distance.

Rendering. Colouring or shading a drawing.

Scale. A method of drawing objects bigger or smaller than they are in real life, and of showing how much they have been enlarged or reduced. The scale is often shown as a *ratio*.

Side view. Two-dimensional drawing of the side of an object, used in *orthographic projection*.

Third angle. Type of *orthographic projection* in which the left-hand *side view* is shown to the left of the *front view*, above which is the *plan*.

Thumbnail sketch. A tiny sketch.

Tone. The degree of lightness or darkness of a colour.

Two-point. Method of *perspective* drawing in which there are two *vanishing points*.

Vanishing point. In *perspective* drawing, a point on the horizon at which the *receding lines* appear to meet.

Index